I0277815

Sole distributors:
Travis & Emery,
17 Cecil Court,
London, WC2N 4EZ,
United Kingdom.
(+44) 20 7 459 2129.
sales@travis-and-emery.com

carlo maria giulini

in memory of susan ann hunt
19 march 1912 - 10 january 2002

discography and concert register compiled by john hunt

contents

7	introduction
21	the discography
89	the concert register
259	selection of philharmonia concert programmes
285	orchestras conducted by carlo maria giulini
286	vocal and instrumental soloists

Carlo Maria Giulini
Published by John Hunt.
Designed by Richard Chluparty
© 2002 John Hunt
reprinted 2009
ISBN 978-1-901395-11-2

acknowledgement
these publications have been made possible by contributions or advance subscriptions from the following

Stefano Angeloni
Yoshihiro Asada
E.C. Blake
Edward Chibas*
Dennis Davis
Richard Dennis
Hans-Peter Ebner*
T.J. Foley
Peter Fülop
Philip Goodman
Johann Gratz
Tadashi Hasegawa*
Andrew Keener
Detlef Kissmann
Elisabeth Legge-Schwarzkopf
John Mallinson*
Philip Moores
W. Moyle
Alan Newcombe
Jim Parsons*
David Patmore*
Tully Potter
Ingo Schwarz
Tom Scragg*
Yoshihiko Suzuki*
Julian Tremayne
Graeme Wright*
Ken Wyman
Koji Kinoshita

Stathis Arfanis
Derek Bevan
Gordon Buffard
Robert Dandois
F. De Vilder
John Derry
Henry Fogel*
Nobuo Fukumoto
Carlos Ginebrada
Jean-Pierre Goossens
Michael Harris*
Naoya Hirabayashi
Rodney Kempster
John Larsen
Douglas MacIntosh
Carlo Marinelli
Bruce Morrison
Alessandro Nava
Hugh Palmer*
Laurence Pateman
James Pearson
Patrick Russell
Robin Scott
Graham Silcock
Michael Tanner
Urs Weber*
Stephen Wright
Ferenc Zemplenyi

*indicates life subscriber

REQUIEM MASS

33⅓

Carlo Maria Giulini: a portrait by Richard Osborne

Dr Johnson once observed of Edmund Burke: "You could not stand five minutes with that man beneath a shed whilst it rained, but you must be convinced you had been standing with the greatest man you had ever yet seen." It wasn't in a shed, and as far as I know it wasn't raining, but it was in Milan in 1951 that Peter Diamand first met Carlo Maria Giulini. Giulini was at that time conductor of the Milan Radio Orchestra. A year or two previously, he had made guest appearances in Strassburg and Prague; but at the relatively advanced age of 37 he was virtually unknown to the wider musical world. Diamand recalls a conversation that seemed to last minutes but in fact lasted hours, on the strength of which he invited Giulini to appear at the Holland Festival. Since Diamand had never heard him conduct a note of music, the board of the Holland Festival was more than a touch *boulversé*. Still, the rest, as they say, is history. Giulini appeared regularly at the Holland Festival until 1965 when Diamand left for Edinburgh, where he again quickly became a prized guest. One year, at Benjamin Britten's request, he conducted the *War Requiem*, a rare foray by Giulini into contemporary repertory.

He is not a musician about whom stories circulate, though Diamand recalls that as a young man Giulini had an ambition to be a circus artist. (Some conductors, you will protest, *are* circus artists.) Nothing seems more improbable, for everyone agrees here is a man of great natural warmth, courteous and soft-spoken. I have often thought of him, as a man and as a musician, as the very embodiment of elegance – not in the sartorial sense of the term (though he is that, too) – but in that valued older sense which indicates mannerliness, cultivated taste, and moral integrity.

And yet what banked-down fires there are within. In his autobiography *My First Forty Years* (Weidenfeld: 1983) Placido Domingo has written: "It would be difficult to find another musician with Giulini's combination of gentleness and intensity. His music-making is extremely refined. In the 'Dies irae' he seemed to personify God the Father on the Day of Judgment. Not that he overacted or made pompous gestures: he simply *became* the music to a frightening degree. It was shocking to see someone who is so good and gentle demonstrate such power, like God on the day of wrath."

Hugh Bean recalls a similarly awesome Victor de Sabata clutching the baton with both hands in the *Dies irae,* bringing it down like an executioner's axe. Was de Sabata a formative influence? It is difficult to say, given the fact that as a young viola player in Rome's legendary Augusteo Orchestra Giulini played under all the great contemporary conductors with the sole and notable exception of Toscanini. Philip Jones, who also played for de Sabata before playing under Giulini in the Philharmonia, remembers things in the latter's repertory of gestures (more particularly to the chorus) that were reminiscent of de Sabata. In other respects, though, they were light years apart. De Sabata, with his terrible blue eyes and fierce manner, was one of the Old School ("the old terrorists" as Jones calls them). Giulini was calmer, gentler, a persuader of men in the modern style.

Hugh Bean has played under Giulini on and off for over 30 years, mostly as Leader. He will tell you that Giulini has never been known to raise his voice in anger. He has no need to. He has his own natural authority. And, in any case, he is a players' man. Is the temperature right? Have the fiddles enough elbow-room? Can the back-desk violas see clearly? He has been known to walk off to recompose himself – in EMI's *Don Giovanni* sessions, for example, when Eberhard Wächter refused to sing out in a balance test. And once, in India at the very end of a gruelling world tour with the Israel Philharmonic, Giulini is said to have tried to separate the leg of an antique chair from its elegantly crafted base when his assistant Gary Bertini appeared for the nth time on the tour to report that the horns were playing too loudly.

Walter Legge dubbed Giulini Saint Sebastian, the suffering one, and there have been times when orchestral players have feared that his only pleasure amid the tension of live music-making was that of reaching the final chord. Yet in those days there was no evidence that he was taking anything other than deep pleasure in the business of music-making.

For the most part, he has side-stepped those aspects of musical life which history suggests bring nothing but trouble. Twice in the last 30 years, he has headed an orchestra. He left the Vienna SO after two years when it became clear that no one was willing to implement changes in personnel; and in Los Angeles, his wife's illness effectively ended what was an altogether happier and more productive experience.

In the 1960s he turned his back on the world's opera houses. At a time when Pierre Boulez was suggesting they should be blown up and Herbert von Karajan, similarly frustrated, was retreating to his Salzburg enclave, Giulini simply retired, irritated beyond recall by jet-lagged singers, militant Trade Unionists, and a new generation of stage directors whose intellectual arrogance was matched only by the general level of their musical ignorance.

The crunch had come in New York in the late 1960s, though Giulini had already had a bad experience at the Holland Festival when 48 hours before the first night of a new production of *Don Giovanni* he no longer felt able to conduct. (In the event, Peter Diamand sacked the director and retained Giulini with a skeletal stage show.) In Milan in the 1950s Giulini had worked with Visconti and the young Zeffirelli. (Promoted by Giulini from design to production when it became clear that Zeffirelli knew the music better than the stage director.) Giulini explains: "Visconti was not only a great film director; he was also steeped in music. By the age of five he was already visiting La Scala. He knew the difference between the straight theatre and opera – that in Verdi's *Otello* it is *Verdi* who is interpreting Shakespeare not the theatre director. The director's job it is to bring into harmony the music, the stage movement, and the interior drama."

Visconti, Giulini, and Callas were fellow spirits, undertaking the most meticulous preparation in a quest for musical and dramatic perfection. In *La traviata* they came very near to achieving it. There is a moment in Act 2 shortly after the arrival of Germont *pere* where Germont's sarcasm is almost too much for Violetta. Diamand recalls that at this point in the La Scala production Callas got up and crossed the room as if to leave. "I saw it four or five times, and every time I was convinced that the curtain would come down – that she was, indeed, going to leave. It was so real, and so human." Not that Giulini always agreed with Callas. He has grim memories of her Rosina ("she was not Rosina, she was Carmen") and is far from happy that an 'unofficial' recording exists of his conducting the production. (De Sabata had dropped out and despite running a fever Giulini was manoeuvred into taking over the performance.)

The La Scala *La traviata* has recently been reissued by EMI; but Giulini's other Verdi recordings are equally important. Pride of place probably goes to the *Don Carlo,* much delayed but eventually recorded by EMI in 1970 a decade after the Visconti production at Covent Garden. And there is also Giulini's fascinatingly autumnal account of *Falstaff* recorded in Los Angeles in 1982. EMI wanted to record *Rigoletto* in 1963 with Mario Sereni in the title-role; but Giulini said no to Sereni and Walter Legge agreed: "This part needs a great tragic artist, not an inoffensive little fellow like the aptly named Sereni." Giulini waited until 1979 and for a cast that included Cappuccilli, Domingo and Cotrubas before finally committing himself to the work. As for his recording of *Il trovatore,* I remember using bits of this to illustrate an interval talk on the opera during a multinational link-up between the New York

Metropolitan and various European TV and radio networks. It was a mistake. It would be an exaggeration to say the BBC switchboards were jammed; but an awful lot of people either rang in or wrote demanding to know the identity of the recording used in the talk. Even in extracted form, it was palpably streets ahead of the transmission itself. The BBC was not amused.

Giulini is not one of those conductors who 'follows' the singer. Graziella Sciutti, who worked a great deal with him in the 1950s and 1960s, testifies to something higher: a state of trust between singer and conductor that diffused tension and allowed the singer's sound to flower naturally. Giulini claims he knows nothing about the voice as a physical instrument. Because it is a human device and not a mechanical one, it requires specialist knowledge matched to a high degree of intuitive awareness. The late chorus master at La Scala, the legendary Roberto Benaglio, had the knowledge and the intuition; and whilst Benaglio was alive, Giulini was not a man to keep a dog and bark himself.

Just how you set about pacing, colouring, and projecting the orchestral part of a Verdi score is something Giulini is reluctant to talk about, perhaps because that, too, is partly a matter of intuition, perhaps because it would take a lifetime to explain. Once, when he was preparing Donizetti's *L'Elisir d'amore* in La Scala, he insisted on the singers varying their declamation in a duet where radically different emotions were being expressed verse by verse in music that was itself unchanging. Afterwards, Toscanini confronted him with the effect. "Why did you do this when the music is the same?" Giulini tried to explain his interpretative responsibility at this point. "You are right," said Toscanini, whose reputation as a literalist was always much exaggerated.

Giulini was not taught conducting, nor does he teach it. (Conductors like Rattle and Myung-Whun Chung will testify to his wisdom, but he would rather meet you with pistols at dawn than admit he taught them anything.) He gives no thought as to how, physically, he conducts and you would surprise him if you attempted to analyse it. In any case, passing judgment on a conductor's beat is a fool's game, unless you happen to be a player or a fellow conductor. (Rostropovich, a great admirer, is deeply interested in Giulini as an example of the potentially compromising 'long arm' symdrome.) Back in 1960, the admirable and erudite Paul Henry Lang wrote in the *New York Herald Tribune*:

"Carlo Maria Giulini is obviously a good musician but he is a 'soft' conductor. His upbeat is leisurely and his downbeat too elaborate to be precise. He looks awkward, flailing a good deal, and in general expends too much energy on conductorial calisthenics."

Hugh Bean does not agree. Giulini's beat, he recalls, was so fiercely incisive in those days (it has mellowed since) it often made an audible swish. Indeed, during the recording of Falla's *The Three-cornered Hat* retakes were required to eliminate the nuisance!

Bean remembers what he calls the persuasive drive of Giulini's conducting, his knowledge of the inner structure of a piece, and his concern for the internal balances of a large symphony orchestra. The typical Giulini sound has about it a warm glow, string based, and never overbalanced by blatant brass. (Philip Jones testifies that Giulini tended to leave the brass severely alone, never asking them to overblow as so many conductors do.) Logic and beauty have always been the order of the day, enlivened by a powerful inner momentum. And that remains the case, even though in some works the tempos have broadened down the years.

A great conductor will release an orchestra's corporate energies without necessarily dictating to the players. In this respect, Beecham was a master, Karajan too, according to Bean. Giulini, though, is subtly different. As soloists like Perlman and Rostropovich have discovered, Giulini is a very focused musician. However prolonged the consultation, Giulini's input into any performance is always, in the final analysis, a strong one.

He was also, from the earliest years, agnostic about the wonderful world of studio technology. The first time he worked for Walter Legge, in Rome on a recording of the Cherubini Requiem, he asked for a supernumary final session to play the piece through complete, as a performance. That is what we have on the LP (the famous *Dies irae* marvellously done) at a time when other musicians were besotted with the arcane niceties of tape editing.

In this sense, Giulini has never been a la mode. (Musically speaking, though not necessarily in more mundane matters. His recording producer Christopher Bishop remembers an absorbed conversation over lunch at the Connaught Hotel in London on the pros and cons of microwaving porridge.) Giulini is also famously choosy about what he conducts, a characteristic that has led to the widely held view that he has 'a small repertory'.

In reality, Giulini's is not so much a small repertory as a frustrating one. Since he has, at one time or another, made a memorable recording of C, we are all too acutely aware that he has omitted to give us A, B or D. Why the *Rhenish*, we ask, but none of the other Schumann symphonies? Why – a less intelligent enquiry, perhaps - Mahler's No. 1 and 9, and nothing in between? The fact is, Giulini will not conduct a work until he has come to know and love every note of it. In the EMI archive there is a Tchaikovsky Fifth by him that ceases shortly after the horn melody in the slow movement. The more he records or conducts, the more we expect him to do. Back in the 1960s, EMI tried coaxing him into recording a work he reveres, Elgar's *The Dream of Gerontius*. After which, no doubt, he would have stood accused of neglecting to record the symphonies.

We live in an age where life on the material level is perhaps as easy as it has ever been. For Giulini's generation it was less so. As Pasternak has it at the end of *Dr Zhivago*: "Living your life is not as easy as crossing a ploughed field". Giulini served with the Italian army in Bosnia before going to ground in Rome in 1943 to avoid the Fascists. War and deprivation scarred his early manhood, just as the Catholic faith he has held to since childhood has helped give his personal and artistic life a measure of wholeness and continuity.

In recent years his wife's illness has made him more introspective. Rostropovich told me: "I have seen the suffering in his face, yet his dedication never wavers. He is a better man than most of us can ever hope to be." Some of this has fed into the music-making. Peter Diamand recalls a recent performance of the *Unfinished* Symphony as fine as any he has heard. But, then, this is not surprising. For Giulini, this symphony (which for him is finished) has always been one of music's great rites of passage.

I asked Giulini whether it is possible successfully to conduct a work like the Verdi Requiem without faith. He said he didn't know. "I have the gift of faith. I believe. So I cannot know what it is like to be without it. Perhaps you can interpret the Requiem as a text." But was his faith not shaken by the atrocities of war? "There are some words with which we always have to struggle: 'if', and 'why?'. I ask myself 'Why is this so....' or 'If there is a God....' I hope one day we will have the answers to these things, but it will not be in this life."

And music: "Music is a form of human expression that on the page is dead. It lives when the first note is sounded and it dies as the final note note dies away. After that comes the applause: beautiful but dangerous. I always say, we must not being the applause home with us; we must leave it there. If it means anything it is not 'Bravo!' but 'Thank you'. My eldest son is a surgeon. He saves life, but he receives no applause. Applause is for the footballer, for the acrobat in the circus. It would be inhuman not to enjoy it. But, please, leave it there. Afterwards, all we can ask is 'How, next time, can we do it better?"

Richard Osborne's portrait was written for Gramophone to mark Giulini's eightieth birthday in 1994; it is reprinted here with the author's permission

John Hunt is also grateful to the following individuals who gave help and suggestions in the compiling of this volume: Richard Chlupaty, Siam Chowkwanyun, Michael Gray, Syd Gray, Bill Holland, Ken Jagger, Roderick Krüsemann, Luis Luna, Alan Newcombe, Malcolm Walker and Nitza Weisgras

ROSSINI
OVERTURES · OUVERTÜREN

L'Italiana in Algeri · Il barbiere di Siviglia
Il signor Bruschino · La scala di seta · La Cenerentola
La gazza ladra · Semiramide · Guglielmo Tell

Philharmonia Orchestra
CARLO MARIA GIULINI

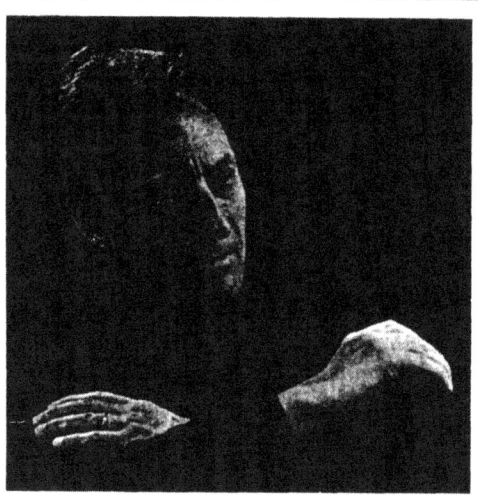

CDM 7 69042 2

carlo maria giulini: the discography

JOHANN SEBASTIAN BACH (1685-1750)

mass in b minor

london 10 july 1972	new philharmonia orchestra and chorus hill baker pears shirley-quirk	cd: bbc legends BBCL 40622 *concert in st paul's cathedral*
munich 2-3 june 1994	bavarian radio orchestra and chorus ziesak alexander van nes k.lewis wilson-johnson	cd: sony S2K 66354

LUDWIG VAN BEETHOVEN (1770-1827)

symphony no 1
milan 8-11 december 1991	la scala philharmonic	cd: sony SK 48236

symphony no 2
milan 8-11 december 1991	la scala philharmonic	cd: sony SK 48238

symphony no 3 "eroica"
los angeles 24-25 november 1978	los angeles philharmonic	lp: dg 2531 123/413 9791 cd: dg 435 0922/447 4442
london 2 may 1980	los angeles philharmonic	unpublished radio broadcast
milan 15-17 november 1992	la scala philharmonic	cd: sony SK 58974
vienna 17 may 1994	vienna philharmonic	unpublished radio broadcast

symphony no 4
milan 17-20 october 1993	la scala philharmonic	cd: sony SK 58921

beethoven **symphony no 5**

los angeles november 1981	los angeles philharmonic	lp: dg 2532 049 cd: dg 410 0282/445 5022
milan 17-20 october 1993	la scala philharmonic	cd: sony SK 58921

symphony no 6 "pastoral"

london 18-20 january 1968	new philharmonia	lp: emi ASD 2535/1C063 02004/ 3C165 52060-52063 lp: angel 36684/32007 cd: royal classics ROY 6403 *recording completed on 23-24 april 1968*
los angeles november 1979	los angeles philharmonic	lp: dg 2531 266 cd: dg 429 3682
milan 27-28 september 1991	la scala philharmonic	cd: sony SK 53974

also an undated video recording of rehearsal performance with a student orchestra

symphony no 7

chicago 29 march 1971	chicago symphony	lp: emi ASD 2737/1C063 02165/ 3C165 52060-52063 lp: angel 36048/32097 cd: emi CDM 769 0312/CZS 575 4622
milan 27-30 september 1991	la scala philharmonic	cd: sony SK 48236

beethoven **symphony no 8**

london 22-29 november 1972	london symphony	lp: emi SLS 841/2C181 02366-02367/ 3C165 52060-52063/1C191 02366-02367 lp: angel 3795 cd: emi CDM 769 0312 cd: royal classics ROY 6403
milan 20-22 september 1992	la scala philharmonic	cd: sony SK 48238

symphony no 9 "choral"

london
22-29
november
1972
	london symphony
	orchestra and
	chorus
	armstrong
	reynolds
	tear
	shirley-quirk
		lp: emi SLS 841/2C181 02366-02367/
		    1C191 02366-02367/1C037 03720/
		    3C165 52060-52063
		lp: angel 3795
		cd: laserlight 16203

berlin 16-17 february 1989	berlin philharmonic ernst-senff-chor varady van nes k.lewis estes	cd: dg 427 6552 *recording completed on 13 february 1990*

piano concerto no 1

vienna 21 september 1979	vienna symphony michelangeli	lp: dg 2531 302 cd: dg 419 2482/447 6432/449 7572 *also unpublished video recording; unofficial* *lp edition also published by rococo*

beethoven **piano concerto no 3**
london   philharmonia   lp: columbia 33CX 1903/SAX 2543
20 april   richter-haaser
1963

vienna   vienna symphony   cd: dg 423 2302/447 6432/449 7572
1 february   michelangeli   *also unpublished video recording*
1979

piano concerto no 5 "emperor"
vienna   vienna symphony   lp: dg 2531 385
1 february   michelangeli   cd: dg 419 2492/447 7572
1979   *also unpublished video recording*

violin concerto
vienna   vienna symphony   cd: live classics best (japan) LCB 101
25 may   oistrakh   *orchestra incorrectly described by live classics*
1974   *best as vienna philharmonic*

london   london   emi unpublished
6-7   philharmonic   *recording not approved by the soloist*
may   perlman
1977

london   philharmonia   lp: emi ASD 4059/1C063 43063/
14-16   perlman   2C069 43060/3C065 43060
september   cd: emi CDC 747 0022/CMS 764 9222/
1980   CDM 566 9002
                                       vhs video: emi MVC 991 0143
                                       laserdisc: emi LDA 991 0141

coriolan overture
milan   la scala   cd: sony SK 53974
17 november   philharmonic
1992

beethoven **egmont overture**

turin 24 march 1961	rai torino orchestra	lp: cetra LAR 46 cd: cetra ARCD 2054
turin 26 january 1968	rai torino orchestra	cd: emi CZS 575 4622
london 28-29 may 1969	new philharmonia	lp: emi ASD 2535/1C063 02004 lp: angel 36684/32007
milan 22 september 1992	la scala philharmonic	cd: sony SK 53974

mass in c

tooting   new philharmonia   lp: emi ASD 2661/1C063 02124/
15-18   orchestra and   2C069 02124/3C065 02124
september   chorus   lp: angel 36775
1970   ameling   cd: emi CZS 762 6932/CMS 566 3292/
              baker   CZS 569 4402
              altmeyer
              rintzler

beethoven **missa solemnis**

london 15 may 1966	new philharmonia orchestra and chorus lorengar veasey r.lewis borg	cd: arkadia CD 527 *also unpublished video recording*
london 16 july 1968	new philharmonia orchestra and chorus zylis-gara höffgen tear arié	cd: bbc legends BBCL 40932 *concert in st paul's cathedral*
rome 20 december 1969	rai roma orchestra prague philharmonic chorus arroyo hamari hollweg el hage	cd: arkadia CD 707/CDGI 707

london
1-10
may
1975
	london philharmonic
	new philharmonia
	chorus
	harper
	baker
	tear
	sotin
		lp: emi SLS 989/1C163 02740-02741/
		    2C167 02740-02741/
		    3C165 02740-02741
		lp: angel 3836
		cd: emi CZS 762 6932/CMS 565 8272/
		    CZS 569 4402

berlin 13 january 1979	berlin philharmonic ernst-senff-chor moser hamari schreier ridderbusch	cd: vip (japan) CD 5005-5006

VINCENZO BELLINI (1801-1835)

i puritani, excerpt (ah per sempre)
turin   rai torino   lp: melodram MEL 657
5 march   orchestra
1951   silveri

HECTOR BERLIOZ (1803-1869)

les nuits d'été, song cycle
london   london philharmonic   cd: bbc legends BBCL 40772
14 may   baker
1975

roméo et juliette, orchestral excerpts (romeo alone; ball at the capulets; love scene; queen mab scherzo; romeo at the tomb)
chicago   chicago symphony   lp: emi ASD 2606/1C063 02067/
september-   2C069 02067/3C065 02067
october   lp: angel 36038/32035
1969   cd: emi CDC 747 6162/CZS 568 5862

GEORGES BIZET (1838-1875)

jeux d'enfants
london	philharmonia	columbia unpublished
2 october		
1955		

london	philharmonia	lp: columbia 33CX 1518/SAX 2279
6-7		lp: angel 35462
october		lp: emi XLP 30067/SXLP 30067
1956		cd: emi CZS 575 4622

carmen, excerpt (la fleur que tu m'avais jetée)
los angeles	los angeles	lp: dg 2532 009
november	philharmonic	cd: dg 400 0302/415 3662/445 5252
1980	domingo	

les pecheurs de perles, excerpt (je crois entendre encore)
los angeles	los angeles	lp: dg 2532 009
november	philharmonic	cd: dg 400 0302/445 5252
1980	domingo	

LUIGI BOCCHERINI (1743-1805)

symphony in c minor

london	philharmonia	lp: columbia 33CX 1539
5-8		lp: angel 35712/32094
october		cd: testament SBT 1155
1956		

turin	rai torino	lp: cetra LAR 46
24 march	orchestra	cd: cetra ARCD 2054
1961		cd: arkadia CDLSMH 34001/ CDMP 411

cello concerto in b flat, arranged by grützmacher

london	philharmonia	lp: columbia 33CX 1665
30 may	starker	lp: columbia (germany) C 91046/ 33WCX 1665
1958		lp: angel 35725
		lp: emi 2M 155 53430-53431/ 1C047 50806
		cd: emi CZS 568 4852/CZS 568 7452

overture in d

london	philharmonia	lp: columbia 33CX 1539
7 october		lp: angel 35712/32094
1956		cd: testament SBT 1155

ALEXANDER BORODIN (1833-1887)

prince igor, excerpt (no rest no sleep)

turin	rai torino	lp: melodram MEL 657
26 november	orchestra	
1951	silveri	
	sung in italian	

JOHANNES BRAHMS (1833-1897)

symphony no 1

london 16-17 january 1961	philharmonia	lp: columbia 33CX 1773/SAX 2420 lp: angel 35835 lp: emi SLS 5241/1C197 53776-53779 cd: emi CZS 252 1682/CDM 252 1322
rome 16 december 1967	rai roma orchestra	unpublished video recording
los angeles november 1981	los angeles philharmonic	lp: dg 2532 056 cd: dg 410 0232/427 8042/431 5912
vienna april 1991	vienna philharmonic	cd: dg 435 3472

symphony no 2

london 10-11 october 1962	philharmonia	lp: columbia 33CX 1855/SAX 2498 lp: columbia (germany) C 91149/STC 91149 lp: emi SLS 5241/1C197 53776-53779 cd: emi CZS 252 1682/CDM 253 6672
los angeles november 1980	los angeles philharmonic	lp: dg 2532 014 cd: dg 400 0662
vienna april 1991	vienna philharmonic	cd: dg 423 3482

symphony no 3

london 12 october 1962	philharmonia	lp: columbia 33CX 1872/SAX 2516 lp: columbia (germany) C 91316/STC 91316 lp: angel 60101 lp: emi SLS 5241/2C053 43099/ 1C197 53776-53779 cd: emi CZS 252 1682/CDM 253 6672 *recording completed on 9-11 november 1962*
vienna may 1990	vienna philharmonic	cd: dg 431 6812

brahms **symphony no 4**

london 22-23 april 1968	new philharmonia	lp: emi SLS 5241/1C197 53776-53779 cd: emi CZS 252 1682/CDM 253 8382 *recording completed on 12 july 1968*
chicago 15 october 1969	chicago symphony	lp: emi ASD 2650/1C063 02083/ 2C069 02083/3C065 02083 lp: angel 36040/32036
vienna 20 may 1989	vienna philharmonic	cd: halloo (japan) HAL 25-26
vienna 20-24 may 1989	vienna philharmonic	cd: dg 429 4032/463 2132
kloster eberbach 29 june 1996	berlin staatskapelle	unpublished video recording *sat 3 television*

piano concerto no 1

london
21-23
april
1960
	philharmonia
	arrau
		lp: columbia 33CX 1739/SAX 2387
		lp: columbia (germany) C 91260/STC 91260
		lp: angel 35892/60264
		lp: emi 1C063 00519/1C187 50266-50277/
		    1C051 00519/1C037 00519/
		    2C069 00519/3C065 00519/
		    CFP 40028
		cd: emi CDM 769 1772/CZS 567 0132

london november 1972	london symphony weissenberg	lp: emi ASD 2992/2C069 12598/ 3C065 12598

brahms **piano concerto no 2**
london   philharmonia   lp: columbia 33CX 1822/SAX 2466
21-22   arrau   lp: columbia (germany) C 91401/SMC 91401
april   lp: angel 60052
1962   lp: emi 1C187 50266-50267/1C037 00568/
                                         2C069 00568/CFP 40034
                                     cd: emi CDM 769 1782/CZS 567 0132

chicago   chicago   cd: chicago symphony orchestra CSO 90/12
28 november   symphony
1977   rubinstein

violin concerto
chicago   chicago   lp: emi ASD 3385/1C063 02899/
november-   symphony   2C069 02899/3C065 02899
december   perlman   lp: angel 37286
1976   cd: emi CDC 747 1662/CDM 566 9772/
                                         CMS 764 9222

haydn variations
london   philharmonia   lp: columbia 33CX 1778/SAX 2424
25-26   lp: columbia (italy) 33QCX 10446/
january   SAXQ 7366
1961   lp: angel 60335
                                     lp: emi SLS 5241/SXLP 30278
                                     cd: emi CZS 252 1682/CDM 253 8382

vienna   vienna   cd: dg 431 6812
may   philharmonic
1990

brahms **tragic overture**

london	philharmonia	lp: columbia 33CX 1872/SAX 2516
12 october		lp: columbia (germany) C 91316/STC 91316
1962		lp: angel 60101
		lp: emi SLS 5241/2C053 43099/
		1C197 53776-53779
		cd: emi CZS 252 1682/CDM 252 1322

vienna	vienna	cd: dg 429 4032/463 2132
20-24	philharmonic	
may		
1989		

ein deutsches requiem

vienna	vienna	cd: dg 423 5742/445 5462/
20-21	philharmonic	449 6002/449 6512
june	vienna opera	
1987	concert choir	
	bonney	
	a.schmidt	

BENJAMIN BRITTEN (1913-1976)

variations and fugue on a theme of purcell
london	philharmonia	lp: columbia 33CX 1915/SAX 2555
2-4		lp: angel 36215
october		lp: emi SXLP 30240/1C053 00588
1962		cd: emi CZS 767 7232

four sea interludes/peter grimes
london	philharmonia	lp: columbia 33CX 1915/SAX 2555
9 october		lp: angel 36215
1962		lp: emi SXLP 30240/1C053 00588
		cd: emi CZS 767 7232

serenade for tenor, horn and strings
chicago	chicago so	lp: dg 2531 199
april	tear	cd: dg 423 2392
1977	clevenger	

les illuminations
london	philharmonia	lp: dg 2531 199
18-19	tear	cd: dg 423 2392
september		
1978		

a war requiem
london	new	cd: bbc legends BBCL 40462
6 april	philharmonia	*melos ensemble and wandsworth choir*
1969	orchestra and	*are directed by britten*
	chorus	
	melos ensemble	
	wandsworth	
	boys choir	
	woytowicz	
	pears	
	wilbrink	

ANTON BRUCKNER (1824-1896)

symphony no 2

vienna	vienna	lp: emi ASD 3146/1C063 02633/
8-10	symphony	2C069 02633/3C065 02633
december		cd: testament SBT 1210
1974		

symphony no 7

vienna	vienna	lp: dg 419 6271
7-10	philharmonic	cd: dg 419 6272/427 3452/
june		445 5532/449 3052
1986		

vienna	vienna	cd: sardana (japan) SACD 132
10 june	philharmonic	
1986		

symphony no 8

vienna	vienna	lp: dg 415 1241
23-30	philharmonic	cd: dg 415 1242/445 5292
may		
1984		

vienna	vienna	cd: sardana (japan) SACD 133-134
29 may	philharmonic	
1984		

bruckner **symphony no 9**

chicago
december
1976
	chicago
	symphony
		lp: emi ASD 3382/SXLP 30546/
		    1C063 02885/1C053 02885/
		    2C069 02885/3C065 02885
		lp: angel 37287
		cd: emi CDC 747 6372/CDM 565 1772

vienna 10-12 june 1988	vienna philharmonic	cd: dg 427 3452
vienna 11 june 1988	vienna philharmonic	cd: sardana (japan) SACD 135
berlin 10 september 1989	berlin philharmonic	unpublished video recording *performed at herbert von karajan memorial concert*

ALFREDO CATALANI (1854-1893)

la wally

milan 7 december 1953	la scala orchestra and chorus tebaldi scotto del monaco guelfi tozzi	lp: historical recording enterprises HRE 382 cd: great operatic performances GOP 734 cd: legato LCD 177

LUIGI CHERUBINI (1760-1842)

requiem in c minor

rome	santa cecilia	lp: columbia 33CX 1075
1952	orchestra	lp: columbia (france) 33FCX 231
	and chorus	lp: columbia (italy) 33QCX 10045
		lp: columbia (germany) 33WCX 1075
		lp: angel 35042
		lp: emi 3C053 01569

giulini's first recording for the columbia label

les abencérages

florence	maggio	lp: mrf records MRF 52
9 may	musicale	lp: cetra LO 66
1956	orchestra	
	and chorus	
	cerquetti	
	misciano	
	roney	
	petri	
	sung in italian	

FREDERIC CHOPIN (1810-1849)

piano concerto no 1
los angeles	los angeles	lp: dg 2531 125/410 9311
november	philharmonic	cd: dg 415 9702/463 6622
1978	zimerman	

piano concerto no 2
london	philharmonia	lp: replica RPL 2469
16 may	rubinstein	cd: arkadia CD 567
1960		cd: bbc legends BBCL 41052

los angeles	los angeles	lp: dg 2531 126
november	philharmonic	cd: dg 415 9702/463 6622
1979	zimerman	

andante spianato et grande polonaise for piano and orchestra
los angeles	los angeles	lp: dg 2531 126/410 9311/419 0541
november	philharmonic	cd: dg 419 0542
1979	zimerman	

DOMENICO CIMAROSA (1749-1801)

gli orazi e i curiazi
milan	rai milano	cd: melodram CDM 29500
13 april	orchestra	
1952	and chorus	
	vercelli	
	simionato	
	spataro	
	del signore	

CLAUDE DEBUSSY (1862-1918)

la mer
london	philharmonia	lp: columbia 33CX 1818/SAX 2463
11-19		lp: columbia (italy) 33QCX 10478
april		lp: columbia (germany) C 91232/STC 91232
1962		lp: angel 35977/32033
		lp: emi SXLP 30146/1C047 00566/ 3C053 00566
		cd: emi CDM 769 1842
		also issued as cd sampler for great recordings of the century series

los angeles	los angeles	lp: dg 2531 264
november	philharmonic	cd: dg 419 4732/427 2132
1979		

amsterdam	concertgebouw	cd: sony SK 66832
23-25	orchestra	
february		
1994		

trois nocturnes (nuages; fetes; sirenes)
london	philharmonia	lp: columbia 33CX 1818/SAX 2463
14-26	orchestra	lp: columbia (italy) 33QCX 10478
april	and chorus	lp: columbia (germany) C 91232/STC 91232
1962		lp: angel 35977/32033
		lp: emi SXLP 30146/1C047 00566/ 3C065 00566
		cd: emi CDM 769 1842
		also issued as cd sampler for great recordings of the century series

prélude a l'apres-midi d'un faune
amsterdam	concertgebouw	cd: sony SK 66832
23-25	orchestra	
february		
1994		

GAETONO DONIZETTI (1797-1848)

dom sébastien
florence	teatro	lp: mrf records MRF 113
2 may	communale	lp: cetra LO 20/DOC 75
1953	orchestra	
	and chorus	
	barbieri	
	poggi	
	neri	
	mascherini	
	sung in italian	

l'elisir d'amore, excerpt (una furtiva lagrima)
los angeles	los angeles	lp: dg 2532 009
november	philharmonic	cd: dg 400 0302/415 3662/
1980	domingo	445 5252/461 0142

la favorita, excerpt (a tanto amor)
turin	rai torino	lp: melodram MEL 657
1952	orchestra	
	silveri	

lucia di lammermoor, excerpt (tombe degl' avi miei)
los angeles	los angeles	lp: dg 2532 009
november	philharmonic	cd: dg 400 0302/445 5252
1980	domingo	

ANTONIN DVORAK (1841-1904)

symphony no 7

london 28-29 april 1976	london philharmonic	lp: emi ASD 3325/1C063 02830/ 2C069 02830/3C065 02830 lp: angel 37270/32086 cd: emi CZS 568 6282
amsterdam 10-12 february 1993	concertgebouw orchestra	cd: sony SX2K 58946

symphony no 8

london 17-18 january 1962	philharmonia	lp: columbia 33CX 1815/SAX 2461 lp: angel 35847/34449 lp: world records T 590/ST 590 cd: emi CZS 568 6282 *recording completed on 25 april 1962*
chicago march 1978	chicago symphony	lp: dg 2531 046 cd: dg 413 9801
amsterdam 13-14 december 1990	concertgebouw orchestra	cd: sony SK 46670

dvorak **symphony no 9 "from the new world"**
london	philharmonia	lp: columbia 33CX 1759/SAX 2405
18-27		lp: columbia (france) CVD 2101
january		lp: angel 60045/34449
1961		lp: emi SXLP 30163/1C053 00529/ 2C053 00529
		cd: emi CDZ 762 5142/CDE 767 7712/ CZS 568 6282
chicago	chicago	lp: dg 2530 881
april	symphony	cd: dg 423 8822/439 7522
1977		
amsterdam	concertgebouw	cd: sony SX2K 58946
7-8	orchestra	
may		
1992		

cello concerto
london	london	lp: emi ASD 3452/1C063 02964/ 2C069 02964/3C065 02964
29 april-	philharmonic	
1 may	rostropovich	lp: angel 37457
1974		cd: emi CDC 749 3062/CMS 565 7012
1975		CMS 567 8072
london	london	vhs video: emi MVP 991 0202
10-11	philharmonic	laserdisc: emi LDB 991 0201
december	rostropovich	
1977		

scherzo capriccioso
london	philharmonia	lp: columbia 33CX 1815/SAX 2461
18-19		lp: angel 35847
april		lp: world records T 590/ST 590
1962		cd: emi CDZ 762 5142/CDE 767 7712/ CZS 568 6282

carnival overture
london	philharmonia	lp: columbia 33CX 1759/SAX 2405
19 january		lp: columbia (france) CVD 2101
1961		lp: angel 60045
		lp: emi SXLP 30163/1C053 00529/ 2C053 00529
		cd: emi CDE 767 7712/CZS 568 6282

GOTTFRIED VON EINEM (1918-1996)

an die nachgeborenen, cantata

new york 24 october 1975	vienna symphony temple choir hamari fischer-dieskau	unpublished video recording *world premiere performance*
vienna 26 october 1975	vienna symphony wiener singverein hamari fischer-dieskau	lp: dg 666 543 *private issue to commemorate thirtieth anniversary of united nations*

MANUEL DE FALLA (1876-1948)

el amor brujo
london	philharmonia	lp: columbia CX 5265/SAX 5265
16-17	de los angeles	lp: angel 36385
october		lp: emi SXLP 30140/CFP 4512/ 2C053 01317
1961		cd: emi CDM 769 0372/CDM 764 7462/ CMS 567 5872
		recording completed in april 1964

croydon	philharmonia	unpublished video recording
april		*concert for bbc television*
1964		

el sombrero de 3 picos, suite
london	philharmonia	lp: columbia 33CX 1694/SAX 2341
25-29		lp: columbia (germany) C 91071/ STC 91071
july		lp: angel 35820
1957		lp: emi SXLP 30140/CFP 4512/ 2C053 01317
		cd: emi CDM 769 0372/CDM 764 7462
		excerpts
		45: columbia SEL 1635/SEL 1679/ ESL 6262/ESL 6284

croydon	philharmonia	unpublished video recording
april		*concert for bbc television*
1964		

noches en los jardinos de espana
croydon	philharmonia	unpublished video recording
april	roll	*concert for bbc television*
1964		

GABRIEL FAURE (1845-1924)

requiem
watford	philharmonia	lp: dg 419 2431
12-14	orchestra	cd: dg 419 2432
march	and chorus	
1986	battle	
	a.schmidt	

CESAR FRANCK (1822-1890)

symphony in d minor

london 29-30 july 1957	philharmonia	lp: columbia 33CX 1589 lp: angel 35641 lp: emi XLP 30055/SXLP 30055 cd: emi CZS 767 7232
berlin 6-7 february 1986	berlin philharmonic	lp: dg 419 6051 cd: dg 419 6052
vienna 12-13 june 1993	vienna philharmonic	cd: sony SK 58958

variations symphoniques pour piano et orchestre

vienna 11-14 june 1993	vienna philharmonic crossley	cd: sony SK 58958

psyché et éros/psyché

london 31 may 1958	philharmonia	lp: columbia 33CX 1589 lp: angel 35641 lp: emi XLP 30055/SXLP 30055 cd: emi CZS 767 7232
berlin 6-7 february 1986	berlin philharmonic	lp: dg 419 6051 cd: dg 419 6052

CHRISTOPH WILLIBALD GLUCK (1714-1787)

alceste
milan	la scala	lp: ed smith UORC 273
4 april	orchestra	lp: historical operatic treasures ERR 136
1954	and chorus	lp: cetra LO 50
	callas	cd: melodram MEL 26026/GM 20019
	gavarini	cd: sakkaris diva 1101-1102
	zampieri	*excerpts*
	silveri	lp: penzance PR 27
	panerai	lp: dei della musica 16
	sung in italian	

iphigénie en tauride
aix	paris	lp: vox PL 8722/OPBX 212
july	conservatoire	lp: pathé DTX 130-132
1952	orchestra	lp: emi 173 1713
	ensemble vocal	
	neway	
	simoneau	
	mollet	
	massard	

CHARLES GOUNOD (1818-1893)

faust, excerpt (avant de quitter ces lieux)
turin	rai torino	lp: melodram MEL 657
26 november	orchestra	
1951	silveri	
	sung in italian	

EDVARD GRIEG (1843-1907)

piano concerto
london	philharmonia	cd: intaglio INCD 7101
25 november	rubinstein	
1963		

JACQUES HALEVY (1799-1862)

la juive, excerpt (quand du seigneur)
los angeles	los angeles	lp: dg 2532 009
november	philharmonic	cd: dg 400 0302/445 5252
1980	domingo	

FRANZ JOSEF HAYDN (1732-1809)

symphony no 94 "surprise"
london 4-5 october 1956	philharmonia	lp: columbia 33CX 1539 lp: angel 35712/32094
munich 25 january 1979	bavarian radio orchestra	unpublished radio broadcast *bayerischer rundfunk*

symphony no 104 "london"
milan 2 march 1965	rai milano orchestra	cd: cetra CDE 1063

cello concerto in d
london 29-30 may 1958	philharmonia starker	lp: columbia 33CX 1665 lp: columbia (germany) C 91046/ 33WCX 1665 lp: angel 35725 lp: emi 2M 155 53430-53431/ 1C047 50806 cd: emi CZS 568 4852

mass no 11 "nelson"
london 1 may 1966	new philharmonia orchestra and chorus lorengar veasey r.lewis shirley-quirk	unpublished video recording

PAUL HINDEMITH (1895-1963)

mathis der maler, symphony
boston	boston	cd: boston symphony orchestra broadcast archives
30 march	symphony	
1974		

FRANZ LISZT (1811-1886)

piano concerto no 1
vienna	vienna	lp: dg 2530 770/415 8391
june	symphony	cd: dg 415 8392
1976	berman	

piano concerto no 2
vienna	vienna	lp: dg 2530 770/415 8391
june	symphony	cd: dg 415 8392
1976	berman	

GUSTAV MAHLER (1860-1911)

symphony no 1

chicago
30 march
1971
	chicago
	symphony
		lp: emi ASD 2722/1C063 02183/
		    2C069 02183/3C065 02183/
		    SXLP 30548/1C053 02183
		lp: angel 36047/32037
		cd: royal classics ROY 6406
		cd: emi CDM 253 6512

symphony no 9

vienna 26 may 1975	vienna symphony	cd: sardana (japan)
chicago 5-6 april 1976	chicago symphony	lp: dg 2707 097 cd: dg 423 9102/463 6092

das lied von der erde

berlin 14 february 1984	berlin philharmonic araiza fassbänder	cd: sardana (japan)
berlin 15-17 february 1984	berlin philharmonic araiza fassbänder	lp: dg 415 4591 cd: dg 415 4592/469 3042

GIANFRANCESCO MALIPIERO (1882-1973)

mondi celesti, for soprano and ten instruments
rome	rai roma	78: cetra CB 20469-20470
1950	chamber	
	orchestra	
	laszlo	

GIACOMO MEYERBEER (1791-1864)

l'africaine, excerpt (o paradis!)
los angeles	los angeles	lp: dg 2532 009
november	philharmonic	cd: dg 400 0302/445 5252
1980	domingo	

DARIUS MILHAUD (1892-1974)

l'apothéose de moliere, suite for chamber orchestta
rome	rai roma	78: cetra CB 20470-20471
1950	chamber	
	orchestra	

WOLFGANG AMADEUS MOZART (1756-1791)

symphony no 36 "linz"
london 19 july 1982	philharmonia	cd: live classics best (japan) LCB 102

symphony no 39
croydon april 1964	philharmonia	unpublished video recording *bbc television*
berlin 14-15 february 1991	berlin philharmonic	cd: sony SK 48064/SMK 89798

symphony no 40
croydon april 1964	philharmonia	unpublished video recording *bbc television*
turin 26 february 1965	rai torino orchestra	cd: cetra CDE 1034 cd: arkadia CDLSMH 34011/CDMP 411 *CDLSMH 34011 incorrectly dated 1960*
london 18 october- 1 november 1965	new philharmonia	lp: decca LXT 6225/SXL 6225/JB 8 lp: london (usa) CS 6479 cd: decca 417 7272/452 8892
salzburg 2 august 1987	vienna philharmonic	cd: halloo (japan) HAL 15
berlin 24-26 may 1991	berlin philharmonic	cd: sony SK 47264/SMK 89798

mozart **symphony no 41 "jupiter"**
croydon april 1964	philharmonia	unpublished video recording *bbc television*
milan 2 march 1965	rai milano orchestra	cd: frequenz 041.012 cd: cetra CDE 1034 cd: arkadia CDLSMH 34011/CDMP 411
london 18 october- 1 november 1965	new philharmonia	lp: decca LXT 6225/SXL 6225/JB 8 lp: london (usa) CS 6479 cd: decca 417 7272/452 8892
berlin 24-26 may 1991	berlin philharmonic	cd: sony SK 47264

sinfonia concertante for four wind soloists and orchestra
chicago 31 march 1977	chicago symphony still brody elliott clevenger	cd: chicago symphony orchestra soloists
berlin 19-20 march 1992	berlin philharmonic schellenberger brandhofer damiano hauptmann	cd: sony SK 48064

mozart **sinfonia concertante for violin, viola and orchestra**
portsmouth philharmonia unpublished video recording
april brainin *bbc television*
1964 schidlof

violin concerto no 3
london philharmonia columbia unpublished
18 october milstein
1962

piano concerto no 9 "jeunehomme"
vienna vienna lp: emi 1C065 16289/2C069 16289
23-25 symphony
june weissenberg
1978

piano concerto no 13
rome rai roma lp: cetra LAR 26
15 december orchestra lp: music masters MJA 1969.2
1951 michelangeli cd: movimento musica 051.050
 cd: cetra CDE 1002/CDAR 2001/AR 01
 cd: hommage 700 1856/700 1850

piano concerto no 20
rome rai roma lp: cetra LAR 26
15 december orchestra cd: movimento musica 051.050
1951 michelangeli cd: cetra CDE 1002/CDAR 2001/AR 02
 cd: curcio CON 01
 cd: notablu 935.1091-1092
 cd: hommage 700 1857/700 1850
 cd: urania awaiting publication

london philharmonia cd: intaglio INCD 7101
25 november rubinstein
1963

piano concerto no 21
vienna vienna lp: emi 1C065 16289/2C069 16289
23-25 symphony
june weissenberg
1978

mozart **piano concerto no 23**

rome	rai roma	lp: cetra LAR 26/TRV 1001
15 december	orchestra	lp: music masters MJA 1969.2
1951	michelangeli	lp: movimento musica 01.070
		lp: cls records RPCL 2002
		cd: cetra CDAR 2004/AR 02
		cd: movimento musica 051.050/011.009
		cd: hommage 700 1857/700 1850
		cd: urania awaiting publication

milan	la scala	lp: dg 423 2871
march	orchestra	cd: dg 423 2872
1987	horowitz	vhs video: dg 072 1153
		laserdisc: dg 072 1151
		video versions also contain rehearsal extracts.

divertimento no 11

chicago	chicago	cd: chicago symphony orchestra CD 00-10
2-3	symphony	
march		
1967		

serenade no 10 for thirteen wind instruments

rome	members of	cd: cetra CDE 1063
16 december	rai roma	
1967	orchestra	

serenade no 13 "eine kleine nachtmusik"

chicago	chicago	cd: chicago symphony orchestra CD 90-02
2-3	symphony	
march		
1967		

vienna	vienna	cd: live classics best (japan) LCB 101
2 june	symphony	
1973		

mozart **requiem mass**

london 8 may 1966	new philharmonia orchestra and chorus lorengar veasey r.lewis shirley-quirk	cd: arkadia CD 527 *also unpublished video recording*

london
16-17
september
1978
	philharmonia
	orchestra
	and chorus
	donath
	ludwig
	tear
	lloyd
		lp: emi ASD 3723/1C065 03431/
		    2C069 03431/3C065 03431
		lp: angel 37600
		cd: laserlight 16212
		cd: emi CDZ 762 5182/CMS 565 8392/
		    CDR 569 8672/CDR 569 9002

walthamstow 19-21 april 1989	philharmonia orchestra and chorus dawson van nes k.lewis estes	cd: sony SK 45577/SKK 60025/ SM2K 61730

thamos könig in ägypten, incidental music

turin 26 february 1965	rai torino orchestra and chorus meneguzzer zilio frascati monreale *sung in italian*	lp: melodram MEL 034 cd: arkadia CDLSMH 34059/CDMP 450

mozart **don giovanni**

london
7-15
october
1959
	philharmonia
	orchestra
	and chorus
	schwarzkopf
	sutherland
	sciutti
	alva
	wächter
	taddei
	frick
		lp: columbia 33CX 1717-1720/
		   SAX 2369-2372
		lp: columbia (france) 33FCX 875-878/
		   SAXF 192-195/CCA 875-878
		lp: columbia (germany) 33WCX 518-521/
		   SAXW 9503-9506/C 91059-91062/
		   STC 91059 91062
		lp: angel 3605
		lp: emi SLS 5083/1C161 00504-00507/
		   1C165 00504-00507/2C165 00504-00507
		cd: emi CDS 747 2608/CDS 556 2322/
		   CMS 567 8692
		excerpts
		lp: columbia 33CX 1918/SAX 2559
		lp: columbia (germany) C 80714/
		   STC 80714
		lp: angel 36948/3754
		lp: emi ASD 2915/SXLP 30300/YKM 5002/
		   1C061 02056/1C037 03069/
		   2C061 02056
		cd: emi CDM 763 0782/CDM 565 5772/
		   CDM 566 5672
		recording completed on 23-24 november 1959

rome 12 may 1970	rai roma orchestra and chorus jurinac janowitz miljakovic kraus ghiaurov bruscantini petkov	cd: melodram MEL 37080 cd: arkadia CDLSMH 34059/CDMP 450 cd: frequenz 043.019 cd: cetra CDAR 2049 cd: rodolphe RPV 32675-32677 cd: opera d'oro 1144 *excerpts* cd: gala GL 100.593

mozart **le nozze di figaro**

london
16-27
september
1959
	philharmonia
	orchestra
	and chorus
	schwarzkopf
	moffo
	cossotto
	wächter
	taddei
		lp: columbia 33CX 1732-1735/
		    SAX 2381-2384
		lp: columbia (france) 33FCX 862-865/
		    SAXF 114-117
		lp: columbia (germany) C 91184-91186/
		    STC 91184-91186
		lp: angel 3608
		lp: emi SLS 5152/1C165 00514-00517/
		    1C147 01751-01753/1C191 03464-03466/
		    2C165 00514-00517/3C165 00514-00517
		cd: emi CMS 763 2662
		excerpts
		lp: columbia 33CX 1934/SAX 2573
		lp: columbia (france) CVT 3558
		lp: columbia (germany) C 80859/SMC 80859
		lp: angel 35640/3754
		lp: emi SXLP 30303/YKM 5002/
		    1C061 01392/2C061 01392/
		    1C063 00839/1C147 30636-30637
		cd: emi CDM 566 0492/CDM 565 5772

london 6 february 1961	philharmonia orchestra and chorus schwarzkopf söderström berganza blanc corena	unpublished radio broadcast
amsterdam 23 june 1961	residentie orchestra netherlands chamber choir schwarzkopf sciutti malagu prey taddei	cd: verona 27092-27094 *excerpts* cd: globe GLO 6900/GLO 6901

MODEST MUSSORGSKY (1839-1891)

pictures from an exhibition, arranged by ravel
edinburgh 7 september 1961	philharmonia	cd: bbc legends BBCL 40232
chicago april 1976	chicago symphony	lp: dg 2530 783/410 8381/415 8441 cd: dg 415 8442/439 5632
berlin 17-19 february 1990	berlin philharmonic	cd: sony SK 45935/SMK 89615/ SMK 60008

also undated video recording of a performance with an unspecified orchestra

night on bare mountain, arranged by rimsky-korsakov
london 29 september 1956	philharmonia	lp: columbia 33CX 1523/SAX 2416 lp: columbia (germany) C 90905 lp: angel 35463 lp: world records T 816/ST 816 *recording completed on 8 october 1956*

GIOVANNI PERGOLESI (1710-1736)

la serva padrona
milan	la scala	lp: columbia 33CX 1340
29 may-	orchestra	lp: columbia (italy) 33QCX 10152
1 june	carteri	lp: angel 35279/60333
1955	rossi-lemeni	lp: emi 2C063 01335

SERGEI PROKOFIEV (1891-1953)

symphony no 1 "classical"
chicago	chicago	lp: dg 2530 783
april	symphony	cd: dg 410 8381
1976		

violin concerto no 1
london	philharmonia	lp: columbia CX 5275/SAX 5275
17-18	milstein	lp: angel 36009
october		lp: emi SXLP 30235
1962		

MAURICE RAVEL (1875-1937)

alborada del gracioso
london	philharmonia	45: columbia SEL 1684/ESL 6288
4 june		lp: columbia 33CX 1694/SAX 2341
1959		lp: columbia (italy) 33QCX 10383/ SAXQ 7284
		lp: columbia (germany) C 91071/ STC 91071/33WCX 1694/SAXW 2341
		lp: angel 35820
		lp: emi SXLP 30198/EMX 412 0761
		cd: emi CZS 767 7232

daphnis et chloé, second suite
london	philharmonia	lp: columbia 33CX 1694/SAX 2341
8-10		lp: columbia (italy) 33QCX 10383/ SAXQ 7284
june		
1959		lp: columbia (germany) C 91071/ STC 91071/33WCX 1694/SAXW 2341
		lp: angel 35820
		lp: emi SXLP 30198/EMX 412 0761
		cd: emi CZS 767 7232

rapsodie espagnole
london	new	lp: columbia CX 5265/SAX 5265
17-18	philharmonia	lp: angel 36385
may		lp: emi EMX 412 0761
1966		
los angeles	los angeles	lp: dg 2531 264/415 8441
november	philharmonic	cd: dg 415 8442/439 5632
1979		

ravel **ma mere l'oye, suite**

london 9-10 october 1956	philharmonia	lp: columbia 33CX 1518/SAX 2279 lp: angel 35462 lp: emi XLP 30067/SXLP 30067
portsmouth april 1964	philharmonia	unpublished video recording *bbc television*
munich 25-26 january 1979	bavarian radio orchestra	cd: emi CZS 575 4622
los angeles november 1979	los angeles philharmonic	lp: dg 2531 164/415 8441 cd: dg 415 8442/439 5632
amsterdam 23-24 november 1989	concertgebouw orchestra	cd: sony SK 46670/SK 66832

pavane pour une infante défunte

london 17-18 may 1966	new philharmonia	lp: columbia CX 5265/SAX 5265 lp: angel 36385 lp: emi EMX 412 0761
watford 12-14 march 1986	philharmonia	lp: dg 419 2431 cd: dg 419 2432
amsterdam 23-25 february 1994	concertgebouw orchestra	cd: sony SK 66832

GIOACHINO ROSSINI (1792-1868)

il barbiere di siviglia

rome 23 april 1954	rai roma orchestra and chorus cadoni monti panerai calabrese cortis	vhs video: bel canto society 0548 *first complete opera transmitted on italian tv*
milan 16 february 1956	la scala orchestra and chorus callas alva gobbi luise rossi-lemeni	lp: mrf records MRF 101 lp: robin hood records RHR 507 lp: estro armonico EA 015 lp: cetra LO 34 lp: melodram MEL 422 cd: melodram MEL 26020/GM 20038 *excerpts* lp: limited edition society 100 lp: historical recording enterprises HRE 219 lp: dei della musica 05 cd: melodram MEL 26026
den haag 19 june 1962	residentie orchestra netherlands chamber choir berganza alva capecchi trama corena	cd: gala GL 100 5792 *excerpts* cd: globe GLO 6901/GLO 6900
rome 1 may 1965	rome opera orchestra and chorus berganza alva panerai montarsolo corena	cd: archivi dell' opera 0465/TO92

rossini **il barbiere di siviglia,** overture

london	philharmonia	45: columbia SEL 1696/ESL 6296
9-10		45: columbia (italy) SEBQ 120/SEBQ 250/
june		SCDQ 2004
1959		lp: columbia 33CX 1726/SAX 2377
		lp: columbia (italy) 33QCX 10414/
		SAXQ 7313
		lp: angel 60138
		lp: emi XLP 30094/SXLP 30094/
		CFP 40379/1C037 00814/
		1C053 00814/2C053 00814/
		2C181 52567-52568/3C033 00590
		cd: emi CDM 769 0422

la cenerentola, overture

london	philharmonia	lp: columbia 33CX 1919/SAX 2560
1 april		lp: angel 60048
1964		lp: emi SXLP 30143/1C037 00814/
		1C053 00814/2C053 00814/
		2C181 52567-52568/3C033 00590/
		3C047 00079
		cd: emi CDM 769 0422
		session for this overture previously held on
		13 april 1962

la cenerentola, excerpt (nacqui all' affano)

den haag	residentie	cd: globe GLO 6901/GLO 6900
30 june	orchestra	
1954	simionato	

la gazza ladra, overture

london	philharmonia	lp: columbia 33CX 1919/SAX 2560
2-3		lp: angel 60048
april		lp: emi SXLP 30143/CFP 40379/
1964		1C037 00814/1C053 00814/
		2C053 00814/2C181 52567-52568/
		3C033 00590/3C047 00079
		cd: emi CDM 769 0422

rossini **guillaume tell, overture**

london	philharmonia	lp: columbia 33CX 1919/SAX 2560
13 december		lp: angel 60048
1962		lp: emi SXLP 30143/CFP 40379/
		1C037 00814/1C053 00814/
		2C053 00814/2C181 52567-52568/
		3C033 00590/SLS 5073
		cd: emi CDM 769 0422

l'italiana in algeri

milan	la scala	lp: columbia 33CX 1215-1216
5-12	orchestra	lp: columbia (italy) 33QCX 10111-10112
august	and chorus	lp: columbia (france) 33FCX 388-389
1954	simionato	lp: columbia (germany) 33WCX 1215-1216
	sciutti	lp: angel 3529/6119
	valletti	lp: emi 3C163 00981-00982
	petri	cd: emi CHS 764 0412

excerpts
lp: emi 3C053 18031

l'italiana in algeri, overture

london	philharmonia	45: columbia SEL 1696/ESL 6296
9 june		45: columbia (italy) SEBQ 104/SEBQ 250
1959		lp: columbia 33CX 1726/SAX 2377
		lp: columbia (italy) 33QCX 10414/
		SAXQ 7313
		lp: angel 60138
		lp: emi XLP 30094/SXLP 30094/
		CFP 40379/1C037 00814/
		1C053 00814/2C053 00814/
		2C181 52567-52568/3C047 00590
		cd: emi CDM 769 0422

rossini **la scala di seta, overture**
london	philharmonia	45: columbia SEL 1696/ESL 6296
21-24		45: columbia (italy) SEBQ 104/SEBQ 250
november		lp: columbia 33CX 1726/SAX 2377
1959		lp: columbia (italy) 33QCX 10414/ SAXQ 7313
		lp: angel 60138
		lp: emi XLP 30094/SXLP 30094/ CFP 40379/1C037 00814/ 1C053 00814/2C053 00814/ 2C181 52567-52568/3C047 00590
		cd: emi CDM 769 0422

semiramide, overture
london	philharmonia	lp: columbia 33CX 1919/SAX 2560
14 december		lp: angel 60048
1962		lp: emi SXLP 30143/CFP 40379/ 1C037 00814/1C053 00814/ 2C053 00814/3C033 00590/ 2C181 52567-52568
		cd: emi CDM 769 0422

il signor bruschino
rome	rai roma	lp: melodram MEL 028
september	orchestra	lp: voce records VOCE 32
1951	noni	
	poli	
	bruscantini	

rossini **il signor bruschino, overture**

london	philharmonia	lp: columbia 33CX 1726/SAX 2377
june		lp: columbia (italy) 33QCX 10414/ SAXQ 7313
1959		lp: angel 60138
		lp: emi XLP 30094/SXLP 30094/ 1C037 00814/1C053 00814/ 2C053 00814/3C047 00590/ 2C181 52567-52568
		cd: emi CDM 769 0422

tancredi, overture

london	philharmonia	lp: columbia 33CX 1919/SAX 2560
3 june		lp: angel 60048
1964		lp: emi SXLP 30143/1C037 00814/ 1C053 00814/2C053 00814/ 2C181 52567-52568/3C047 00079
		cd: emi CZS 575 4622

CAMILLE SAINT-SAENS (1835-1921)

cello concerto no 1

london 16-17 september 1957	philharmonia starker	lp: columbia 33CX 1579 lp: columbia (france) 33FCX 323 lp: angel 35598/60266 lp: world records T 529/ST 529 lp: emi 2N155 53430-53431 cd: emi CZS 568 4852
london 29 april- 1 may 1974	london philharmonic rostropovich	lp: emi ASD 3452/1C063 02964/ 2C069 02964/3C065 02964 lp: angel 37457 cd: emi CDC 749 3062
london 10-11 december 1977	london philharmonic rostropovich	vhs video: emi MVP 991 0202 laserdisc: emi LDB 991 0201

ALESSANDRO SCARLATTI (1660-1725)

il trionfo dell' onore

milan 1950	rai milano orchestra zerbini zareska pini berdini poli boriello	lp: cetra LPC 1223 lp: cetra (france) CS 529-530

FRANZ SCHUBERT (1797-1828)

symphony no 4 "tragic"

rome 22 december 1967	rai roma orchestra	cd: cetra CDE 1057
edinburgh 31 august 1968	new philharmonia	cd: bbc legends BBCL 40392
chicago march 1978	chicago symphony	lp: dg 2531 047 cd: dg 429 3682

symphony no 8 "unfinished"

london 27 january 1961	philharmonia	lp: columbia 33CX 1778/SAX 2424 lp: columbia (italy) 33QCX 10446/ SAXQ 7366 lp: angel 60335 lp: emi SXLP 30278
chicago march 1978	chicago symphony	lp: dg 2531 047 cd: dg 423 8822/429 3682/ 439 7522/463 6092

schubert **symphony no 9 "great"**
chicago   chicago   lp: dg 2530 882/419 1081
8-9   symphony
april
1977

munich   bavarian   cd: sony SK 53971
27-28   radio orchestra
february
1993

mass in e flat
edinburgh   new   cd: bbc legends BBCL 40292
31 august   philharmonia
1968   scottish
                 festival chorus
                 pashley
                 michelow
                 hughes
                 robertson
                 mccue

munich   bavarian radio   cd: sony SK 69290
24-28   orchestra
april   and chorus
1995   ziesak
                 van nes
                 lippert
                 bünten
                 schmidt

ROBERT SCHUMANN (1810-1856)

symphony no 3 "rhenish"

london 3-4 june 1958	philharmonia	lp: columbia 33CX 1662 lp: angel 35753 cd: emi CZS 575 4622 *this performance used the re-orchestration by gustav mahler*
turin 24 march 1961	rai torino orchestra	cd: arkadia CDLSMH 34013 cd: cetra CDE 1057
los angeles december 1980	los angeles philharmonic	lp: dg 2532 040 cd: dg 400 0622/427 8182/445 5022
kloster eberbach 29 june 1996	berlin staatskapelle	unpublished video recording *sat 3 television*

schumann **piano concerto**

chicago
8 march
1967
	chicago
	symphony
	rubinstein
		lp: victor LSC 2997/RB 6747/SB 6747/
		    CRL7-0725/RL 43195
		cd: rca/bmg RC 62552/RD 86255/
		    09026 626772/09026 630532

vienna 21-26 may 1992	vienna philharmonic kissin	cd: sony SK 52567

cello concerto

london 17 september 1957	philharmonia starker	lp: columbia 33CX 1579 lp: columbia (france) 33FCX 323 lp: angel 35598/60266 lp: emi 2M155 53430-53431 lp: world records T 529/ST 529 cd: emi CZS 568 4852

manfred overture

london 2 june 1958	philharmonia	lp: columbia 33CX 1662 lp: angel 35753 cd: emi CZS 767 7232
los angeles november 1981	los angeles philharmonic	lp: dg 2532 040 cd: dg 400 0622/427 8042/447 4442

also undated video recording of performance with an unspecified orchestra

JOHANN STRAUSS (1825-1899)

kaiserwalzer

vienna 14 april 1974	vienna symphony	cd: emi CZS 575 4622

IGOR STRAVINSKY (1882-1971)

l'oiseau de feu, 1919 suite

london 1-3 october 1956	philharmonia	lp: columbia 33CX 1518/SAX 2279 lp: angel 35462 lp: emi XLP 30067/SXLP 30067 cd: emi CZS 575 4622 *excerpts* 45: columbia SEL 1635/ESL 6262

chicago
september
1969
	chicago
	symphony
		lp: emi ASD 2614/1C063 02070/
		    2C069 02070/3C065 02070/
		    102 0701
		lp: angel 36039

amsterdam november 1989	concertgebouw orchestra	cd: sony SK 45935

petrushka

chicago
october
1969
	chicago
	symphony
		lp: emi ASD 2614/1C063 02070/
		    2C069 02070/3C065 02070/
		    102 0701
		lp: angel 36039

PIOTR TCHAIKOVSKY (1840-1893)

symphony no 2 "little russian"
london	philharmonia	lp: columbia 33CX 1523/SAX 2416
27-29		lp: columbia (germany) C 90905
september		lp: angel 35463
1956		lp: world records T 816/ST 816
		lp: emi SXLP 30506
		cd: emi CZS 767 7232

symphony no 5
london	philharmonia	columbia unpublished
26 april		*recording incomplete*
1962		

symphony no 6 "pathétique"
london	philharmonia	lp: columbia 33CX 1716/SAX 2368
2-4		lp: angel 60031
june		lp: world records T 634/ST 634
1959		lp: emi SXLP 30208/3C053 01210
		cd: emi CDZ 762 6032/CDE 767 7892

edinburgh	philharmonia	cd: bbc legends BBCL 40232
7 september		
1961		

los angeles	los angeles	lp: dg 2532 013
november	philharmonic	cd: dg 400 0292/427 8232/431 6022
1980		

francesca da rimini
london	philharmonia	lp: columbia 33CX 1840/SAX 2483
10-11		lp: columbia (italy) 33QCX 10485
april		lp: angel 35980/60311
1962		lp: emi SXLP 30509

romeo and juliet, fantasy overture
london	philharmonia	lp: columbia 33CX 1840/SAX 2483
9-10		lp: columbia (italy) 33QCX 10485
april		lp: angel 35980/60311
1962		cd: emi CDC 747 6162/CDE 767 7892

GIUSEPPE VERDI (1813-1901)

aida, excerpt (celeste aida)
los angeles november 1980	los angeles philharmonic domingo	lp: dg 2532 009 cd: dg 400 0302/445 5252

attila
venice 12 september 1951	teatro fenice orchestra and chorus mancini penno guelfi tajo	lp: cls records ARPCL 22024 lp: ed smith EJS 132 cd: voci d'oro 4703

don carlo
london 12 may 1958	covent garden orchestra and chorus brouwenstijn barbieri vickers gobbi christoff	lp: paragon DSV 52008 lp: discoreale 10063-10065 cd: myto MCD 94197 *excerpts* lp: melodram MEL 435

london
august
1970
	covent garden orchestra
	ambrosian opera chorus
	caballé
	verrett
	domingo
	milnes
	raimondi
		lp: emi SLS 956/1C165 02149-02152/
		    2C165 02149-02152/
		    3C165 02149-02152/EX 29 07123
		lp: angel 3774
		cd: emi CDS 747 7018/CMS 567 4012
		excerpts
		lp: emi ASD 2823/1C063 02359/
		    2C069 02359/3C065 02359
		lp: angel 34060
		cd: emi CDM 763 0892

verdi **i due foscari**

milan	rai milano	lp: cls records ARPCL 22021
4 december	orchestra	lp: cetra LAR 21
1951	and chorus	cd: cetra CDAE 2022
	vitale	cd: nuova era NE 2278-2279
	bergonzi	cd: cantus classics CACD 500159
	berzieri	*also issued on lp by morgan records*
	guelfi	

ernani, excerpts (come rugiada al cespite; dell' esilio nel dolore; o tu che l'alma adora)

los angeles	los angeles	lp: dg 2532 009
november	philharmonic	cd: dg 400 0302/445 5252
1980	wagner chorale	*come rugiada al cespite*
	domingo	cd: dg 459 6552

verdi **falstaff**

den haag 20 june 1963	concertgebouw orchestra netherlands chamber choir ligabue cardoni freni barbieri alva corena cappecchi	cd: verona 27095-27096 *excerpts* cd: globe GLO 6901/GLO 6900
los angeles 13-27 april 1982	los angeles philharmonic los angeles master chorale ricciarelli boozer hendrixs valentini-terrani gonsalez bruson nucci	lp: dg 2741 020 cd: dg 410 5032/459 0702
london 30 june 1982	covent garden orchestra and chorus ricciarelli boozrt hendrixs valentini-terrani gonsalez bruson nucci	vhs video: pioneer 84064/23119 vhs video: castle CV1 2001 vhs video: bel canto society F 2035 *excerpts* vhs video: castle CV1 2065

verdi **la forza del destino, overture**

london	philharmonia	lp: columbia 33CX 1726/SAX 2377
1 june		lp: emi XLP 30094/SXLP 30094/
1958		2C181 52567-52568

rigoletto

rome	rome opera	lp: estro armonico EA 020
19 november	orchestra	cd: curcio OP 2
1966	and chorus	cd: innovations GJ 824
	scotto	cd: butterfly BMCD 001
	bartoluzzi	cd: arkadia CDMP 468
	pavarotti	
	paskalis	
	washington	
vienna	vienna	lp: dg 2740 225
3-12	philharmonic	cd: dg 415 2882/457 7532
september	vienna opera	*excerpts*
1979	chorus	lp: dg 2537 057
	cotrubas	cd: dg 423 1142
	obratszowa	
	domingo	
	cappuccilli	
	ghiaurov	

verdi **la traviata**

milan 28 may 1952	rai milano orchestra and chorus tebaldi prandelli orlandi	lp: stradivarius STR 1001-1002 lp: great operatic performances GOP 29 cd: legato SRO 810 cd: istituto discografico italiano IDIS 6367-6368 *stradivarius edition incorrectly dated 1956*
milan 28 may 1955	la scala orchestra and chorus callas di stefano bastianini	lp: mrf records MRF 87 lp: cetra LO 28 lp: discocorp RR 474 lp: morgan MOR 5501 lp: foyer FO 1003 cd: arkadia CD 501/CDHP 501 cd: laudis CF 2001 cd: priceless D 169 cd: amplitude HRCDO 28501 cd: emi CMS 763 6282/CMS 566 4502 *excerpts* lp: dei della musica 01 cd: foyer CDS 14004/CDS 15002/ CDS 15006 cd: myto MCD 89003 cd: memories HR 4372-4373/HR 4400-4401 cd: hallmark 390362/311102 cd: emi CDM 763 4232

milan
19 january
1956
	la scala
	orchestra
	and chorus
	callas
	raimondi
	bastianini
		lp: historical recording enterprises
		   HRE 272
		cd: myto MCD 89003
		excerpts
		lp: historical recording enterprises
		   HRE 219
		lp: dei della musica 01
		cd: arkadia CD 501/CDHP 501
		cd: laserlight 15096

london 19 april 1967	covent garden orchestra and chorus freni cioni cappuccilli	cd: frequenz 043.006 cd: rodolphe RPV 32112-32113

verdi la traviata, preludes to acts 1 and 3

london	philharmonia	lp: columbia 33CX 1726/SAX 2377
31 may-		lp: emi XLP 30094/SXLP 30094/
2 june		2C181 52567-52568
1958		

il trovatore

london	covent garden	lp: legendary LR 175
26 november	orchestra	
1964	and chorus	
	jones	
	simionato	
	prevedi	
	glossop	
	rouleau	

rome	santa cecilia	lp: dg 413 3551
january	orchestra	cd: dg 413 3552/423 8582
1984	and chorus	*excerpts*
	plowright	lp: dg 415 2851
	fassbänder	cd: dg 415 2852/457 9082
	domingo	
	zancanaro	
	nesterenko	

il trovatore, excerpt (ah si ben mio/di quella pira)

los angeles	los angeles	lp: dg 2532 009
november	philharmonic	cd: dg 400 0302/445 5252
1980	domingo	

i vespri siciliani, overture

london	philharmonia	lp: columbia 33CX 1726/SAX 2377
1 june		lp: emi XLP 30094/SXLP 30094/
1958		2C181 52567-52568

london	philharmonia	cd: bbc legends BBCL 40292
7 august		
1963		

croydon	new	unpublished video recording
3 march	philharmonia	*bbc television*
1968		

verdi **messa da requiem**

london 5 august 1963	philharmonia orchestra and chorus shuard reynolds r.lewis ward	cd: bbc legends BBCL 40292
london 16-24 september 1963	philharmonia orchestra and chorus schwarzkopf ludwig gedda ghiaurov	lp: emi AN 133-134/SAN 133-134/ SLS 909/A 91353-91354/ STA 91353-91354/ 1C165 00029-00030/ 2C167 00029-00030/ 3C165 00029-00030 lp: angel 3649 cd: emi CDS 747 2578/CMS 566 2502/ CMS 567 5602 *excerpts* lp: emi HQS 1407/YKM 5015 *recording completed on 7 april 1964*
london 26 april 1964	philharmonia orchestra and chorus ligabue bumbry konya arié	unpublished video recording *music performance research centre*
berlin 29 april- 1 may 1989	berlin philharmonic ernst-senff-chor sweet quivar cole estes	cd: dg 423 6742

verdi messa da requiem/concluded
turin 10 january 1998	rai national orchestra chorus of orchestre de paris dragone lytting neill mikulas	unpublished radio broadcast

4 pezzi sacri

london
10-13
december
1962
	philharmonia
	orchestra
	and chorus
	baker
		lp: emi AN 120/SAN 120/A 91286/
		    STA 91286/1C065 00016/
		    2C069 00016/3C065 00016/
		    SXLP 30508/1C053 00016
		lp: columbia (italy) 33QCX 10487/
		    SAXQ 7370
		lp: angel 36125
		cd: emi CDS 747 2578/CMS 566 2502/
		    CMS 567 5602

croydon 3 march 1968	new philharmonia orchestra and chorus	unpublished video recording *bbc television*
berlin 7-8 september 1990	berlin philharmonic ernst-senff-chor sweet	cd: sony SK 46491/SMK 89619/ SM2K 61730

te deum/4 pezzi sacri

turin 18 may 1962	rai torino orchestra and chorus	cd: arkadia CDLSMH 34026/CDMP 426 *CDLSMH 34026 incorrectly described performers* *as rai roma orchestra and chorus*

ANTONIO VIVALDI (1678-1741)

le 4 stagioni
london	philharmonia	lp: columbia 33CX 1365
29 september-	parikian	lp: columbia (italy) 33QCX 10215
2 october		lp: columbia (france) 33FCX 525/TRI 31110
1955		lp: angel 35216
		cd: testament SBT 1155

l'autunno/le 4 stagioni
london	philharmonia	cd: testament SBT 1155
30 september-	parikian	*unpublished columbia stereo test recording*
1 october		
1955		

credo in e minor for chorus and orchestra
berlin	berlin	cd: sony SK 46491/SMK 89619/
16 september	philharnonic	SM2K 61730
1991	ernst-senff-chor	

gloria in d for soprano, mezzo, chorus and orchestra
amsterdam	concertgebouw	unpublished radio broadcast
22 june	orchestra	*recording incomplete*
1960	omroep chorus	
	schwarzkopf	
	boese	

CARL MARIA VON WEBER (1786-1826)

euryanthe
florence	maggio	lp: cetra DOC 71
9 may	musicale	
1954	orchestra	
	and chorus	
	wilfert	
	borkh	
	a.welitsch	
	kamann	

der freischütz, overture
london	new	emi unpublished
28-29	philharmonia	
may		
1969		

ANTON WEBERN (1883-1945)

5 pieces for small orchestra
amsterdam	concertgebouw	cd: globe GLO 6905/GLO 6900
9 june	orchestra	
1979		

Gustav Mahler
SYMPHONIE NO. 9
Chicago Symphony Orchestra
Carlo Maria Giulini

Giulini

conducting the
PHILHARMONIA ORCHESTRA

L'oiseau de feu — Revised Suite (1919) — *Stravinsky;*
Jeux d'enfants — Suite — *Bizet;*
Ma mère l'oye — Suite — *Ravel*
33CX1515

Symphony in D minor — *Franck;*
Psyché et Eros — *Franck*
33CX1539

Symphony in C minor;
Overture in D — *Boccherini;*
Symphony No. 94 in G ('Surprise') — *Haydn*
33CX1539

I concerti delle stagioni ('The Seasons') — *Vivaldi*
33CX1536

Symphony No. 2 in C minor ('Little Russian')
Tchaikovsky;
A night on the Bare Mountain
Moussorgsky orch. Rimsky-Korsakov
33CX1523

COLUMBIA
(Regd. Trade Mark of Columbia Graphophone Co. Ltd.)
33⅓ R.P.M. LONG PLAYING RECORDS
E.M.I. Records Limited, 8-11 Great Castle Street, London, W.1

Festival of the City of London

Artistic Director Ian Hunter

8-20 July 1968

St Paul's Cathedral
by kind permission of the Dean and Chapter
Friday 19 July at 8 pm

New Philharmonia Orchestra
led by Jack Rothstein
Carlo Maria Giulini *conductor*

Verdi: Requiem

Luisa Bosabalian *soprano*
Julia Hamari *mezzo*
Aldo Bottion *tenor*
Rafael Arie *bass*

New Philharmonia Chorus
Wilhelm Pitz *chorus master*

carlo maria giulini: concert register

rome
july-august
1944
santa cecilia orchestra

purcell suite for strings/liadov enchanted lake/salviucci introduzione passacaglia e finale/brahms symphony 4

rome
7 january 1945
santa cecilia orchestra

cimarosa matrimonio segreto overture/hindemith cello concerto/brahms symphony 2
mainardi, cello

rome
15 january 1945
santa cecilia orchestra

weber freischütz overture/parodi preludio ad una comedia/debussy la mer

naples
13 february 1945
orchestra da camera napoletana

works by corelli, haydn, honegger, hindemith and falla
amfiteatrof, cello

florence
8 april 1945
maggio musicale orchestra

weber freischütz overture/beethoven violin concerto/debussy la mer/berlioz carnaval romain overture
de vito, violin

rome
15 april 1945
santa cecilia orchestra

programme included
bloch schelomo
amfiteatrof, cello

rome
9 may 1945
santa cecilia orchestra

bach air from suite 3/mendelssohn violin concerto/schubert symphony 8/falla el amor brujo
d'albore, violin

rome
11 may 1945
santa cecilia orchestra

bach programme
brandenburg concerti 1, 2 and 3/concerto for two harpsichords
vignanelli and saffi, harpsichords

rome
15 may 1945
santa cecilia orchestra

bach programme
brandenburg concerti 4, 5 and 6/concerto for two violins
belardinelli and ruotolo, violins

florence
25 november 1945
maggio musicale

brahms symphony 4/ravel ma mere l'oye/hindemith mathis der maler symphony

rome
12 march 1947
santa cecilia orchestra

dvorak serenade for strings/busoni sarabande und cortege/davico offerta lirica for soprano and orchestra/beethoven symphony 6
corsi

rome
7 may 1947
santa cecilia orchestra

dvorak symphony 9/jachino fantasia/schumann cello concerto
mazzacurati, cello

turin
23 may 1947
rai torino orchestra

schubert symphony 5/ghedini concerto dell' albatro/franck symphony in d minor

rome
3 december 1947
santa cecilia orchestra

gabrieli canzon quarti toni/berg violin concerto/brahms symphony 4
emanuele, violin

rome
22 february 1948
santa cecilia orchestra
and chorus

bach-respighi nun komm der heiden heiland/renzi vexilla regis/tchaikovsky symphony 2/borodin polovtsian dances

bologna
16 april 1948
teatro communale orchestra

brahms symphony 2/chopin piano concerto 2/ravel daphnis et chloé second suite
uninsky, piano

naples
23 may 1948
san carlo orchestra

works by bach, beethoven, davico and tchaikovsky
gieseking, piano

turin
23 july 1948
rai torino orchestra

bonporti concerto op 11 no 6/tchaikovsky symphony no 2/salviucci introduzione passacaglia e finale/mussorgsky-ravel pictures at an exhibition

capri
14 september 1948
rai torino orchestra

concerti by marini, jacchini, manfredini, stradella, gasparini and bonporti

rome **16 january 1949** santa cecilia orchestra	manfredini sinfonia di chiesa/salviucci introduzione passacaglia e finale/brahms tragic overture/mussorgsky khovantschina prelude/mussorgsky-ravel pictures at an exhibition
florence **17 february 1949** maggio musicale orchestra	manfredini sinfonia di chiesa/beethoven violin concerto/salviucci introduzione passacaglia e finale/tchaikovsky symphony 2 *taschner, violin*
venice **12 march 1949** la fenice orchestra	manfredini sinfonia di chiesa/dvorak symphony 9/franck psyché et éros/mussorgsky-ravel pictures at an exhibition
bologna **7 april 1949** teatro communale orchestra	manfredini sinfonia di chiesa/berg violin concerto/brahms symphony 4 *emanuele, violin*
venice **6 october 1949** la fenice orchestra	pizzetti fedra/tchaikovsky violin concerto/brahms symphony 2 *ferraresi, violin*
rome **22 october 1949** santa cecilia orchestra	brahms symphony 2/pizzetti fedra/weber freischütz overture
rome **14 november 1949** rai roma orchestra	
milan **10 february 1950** rai milano orchestra	manfredini sinfonia di chiesa/khachaturian violin concerto/zafred canto del corso/mussorgsky-ravel pictures at an exhibition *luzzato, violin*

rome
22 march 1950
santa cecilia orchestra

mozart eine kleine nachtmusik/de paoli gaelic songs/
schubert-ghedini string quintet

rome
26 march 1950
santa cecilia orchestra
and chorus

boccherini overture in d/zafred canto del corso/
cherubini requiem in c minor

florence
2 april 1950
maggio musicale
orchestra and
chorus

ghedini messa del venerdi santi
brandi/pirazzini/viaro/corena

florence
6 april 1950
maggio musicale
orchestra

weber freischütz overture/malipiero symphony 4/
brahms symphony 2

bologna
11 may 1950
teatro communale
orchestra and
chorus

mozart symphony 35/bach violin concerto
bwv1042/cherubini requiem in c minor
odnoposoff, violin

venice
20 may 1950
la fenice orchestra

boccherini overture in d/liadov enchanted lake/
tchaikovsky piano concerto 1/debussy la mer
ciccolini, piano

naples
24 may 1950
san carlo orchestra

works by perotti, weber and tchaikovsky
rubinstein, piano

venice
8 june 1950
la fenice orchestra

monteverdi-malipiero sinfonie e ritornelli/
marcello oboe concerto/vivaldi concerto rv535/
wolf-ferrari 4 rusteghi intermezzo/mussorgsky-
ravel pictures at an exhibition
riedmiller, oboe

rome
28 june 1950
santa cecilia orchestra
and chorus

rossini italiana in algeri overture/salviucci
introduzione passacaglia e finale/cherubini
requiem in c minor

rome
28 july 1950
rai roma orchestra

venice　　　　　　　　　peragallo piano concerto/turchi piccolo concerto
11 september 1950　　　notturno/zafred symphony 4
rai roma orchestra　　　　　*michelangeli, piano*
　　　　　　　　　　　　　　concert for the venice biennale of contemporary music

turin　　　　　　　　　　monteverdi il combattimento di tancredi e clorinda
15 october 1950
rai torino orchestra

turin　　　　　　　　　　torelli concerti op 8 nos 3 and 4/desderi cantata
18 october 1950　　　　　for baritone, chorus and orchestra
rai torino orchestra　　　　　*fioravanti*
and chorus

turin　　　　　　　　　　operatic overtures, intermezzi and arias
5 march 1951　　　　　　 *nicolai/silveri*
rai torino orchestra

milan　　　　　　　　　　boccherini overture in d/rota harp concerto/
9 march 1951　　　　　　 turchi piccolo concerto notturno/brahms
rai milano orchestra　　　　　symphony 2
　　　　　　　　　　　　　　aldovandri, harp

milan　　　　　　　　　　haydn il mondo della luna
march 1951　　　　　　　 *concert performance*
rai milano orchestra
and chorus

florence　　　　　　　　　bach-respighi nun komm der heiden heiland/
1 april 1951　　　　　　　labrocha 3 cantate/mussorgsky khovantschina
maggio musicale　　　　　　 prelude/mussorgsky-ravel pictures at an exhibition
orchestra and　　　　　　　 *bruscantini*
chorus

rome　　　　　　　　　　 haydn symphony 49/turchi piccolo concerto
18 april 1951　　　　　　 notturno/schubert mass in e flat
santa cecilia orchestra　　　　*rossi/pavoni/pirino/besma/engst*
and chorus

venice
5 may 1951
la fenice orchestra

bonporti-barblan concerto grosso in a/brahms concerto 2/dvorak symphony 8
arrau, piano

milan
11 may 1951
rai milano orchestra

mozart piano concerto 25/pergallo piano concerto/ beethoven piano concerto 5
michelangel, pianoi

turin
16 may 1951
rai torino orchestra

turchi piccolo concerto notturno/rota harp concerto
aldovandri, harp

strassburg
18 june 1951
rai torino orchestra
and chorus

operatic overtures, arias and choruses/verdi 3 pezzi sacri
tebaldi

venice
12 september 1951
rai milano orchestra
and chorus

verdi attila
mancini/penno/tajo/guelfi
concert performance to mark fiftieth anniversary of the composer's death

milan
17 september 1951
rai milano orchestra
and chorus

programme and soloists as for 12 september

milan
6 and 8 october 1951
la scala orchestra

bonporti concerto op 11 no 8/zafred sinfonia in onore della resistenza/brahms symphony 2

bergamo
18 october 1951
teatro donizetti
orchestra and chorus

verdi la traviata
tebaldi/prandelli/fabbri

bergamo
20 and 23
october 1951
teatro donizetti
orchestra and chorus

verdi la traviata
callas/prandelli/fabbri

milan
27 october 1951
la scala orchestra

bonporti concerto op 11 no 8/brahms symphony 2/
mussorgsky khovantschina prelude/mussorgsky-
ravel pictures at an exhibition

milan
31 october 1951
la scala orchestra

bonporti concerto op 11 no 8/brahms symphony 2/
mussorgsky-ravel pictures at an exhibition/verdi
forza del destino overture

brescia
6 november 1951
la scala orchestra

boccherini overture in d/brahms symphony 2/
mussorgsky-ravel pictures at an exhibition/verdi
forza del destino overture

verona
12 november 1951
la scala orchestra

bach-respighi nun komm der heiden heiland/
brahms symphony 2/mussorgsky-ravel pictures
at an exhibition/verdi forza del destino overture

milan
23 november 1951
rai milano orchestra

ghedini concerto for flute and violin/turchi
piccolo concerto notturno/schubert-mortari
divertissement hongroise

turin
26 november 1951
rai torino orchestra

operatic overtures and arias
tebaldi/silveri

milan
4 december 1951
rai milano orchestra
and chorus

verdi i due foscari
vitale/bergonzi/guelfi

rome
15 december 1951
rai roma orchestra

milan
21 december 1951
rai milano orchestra

scarlatti concerto in f/brahms double concerto/
debussy la mer/borodin polovtsian dances
pelliccia, violin and mainardi, cello

milan
16 february 1952
la scala orchestra
and chorus

falla la vida breve
aranjo/albanese/montarsolo
performed in double bill with mascagni cavalleria rusticana
not conducted by giulini; nine further performances given

milan
10 march 1952
rai milano orchestra
and chorus

arias and duets from verdi la traviata
tebaldi/prandelli

milan
13 april 1952
rai milano orchestra
and chorus

cimarosa gli orazi e i curiazi
vercelli/simionato/spataro/del signore

rome
4 may 1952
rai roma orchestra

malipiero il finto arlecchino
rizzoli/renzi/giorgetti/frascati

milan
9 may 1952
rai milano orchestra
and chorus

beethoven prometheus overture/mendelssohn
piano concerto 1/cherubini requiem in c minor
caporali, piano

milan
28 may 1952
rai milano orchestra
and chorus

verdi la traviata
tebaldi/prandelli/orlandi

florence
21, 22 and 24
june 1952
maggio musicale
orchestra and chorus

cavalli didone
petrella/radev/ziliani/campora

milan
11 july 1952
rai milano orchestra
and chorus

ghedini lord inferno
pagliughi/elmo/carlin/capecchi

aix **26 and 30 july 1952** paris conservatoire orchestra and ensemble vocal de paris	gluck iphigénie en tauride *neway/mollet/simoneau/massard*
rome **27 july 1952** rai roma orchestra	savinio cristoforo colombo *date given may be the date on which the recorded performance was transmitted*
parma **12 september 1952** la scala orchestra	cimarosa matrimonio segreto overture/beethoven symphony 6/mussorgsky-ravel pictures at an exhibition/verdi forza del destino overture
venice **21 and 22 september 1952** la fenice orchestra and chorus	galuppi la diavolessa *noni/rizzieri/cadoni/orlandini/bruscantini/calabrese*
venice **22 october 1952** la fenice orchestra	geminiani concerto op 3 no 2/chopin piano concerto 2/tchaikovsky symphony 2 *marzorati, piano*
milan **18 january 1953** rai milano orchestra	bartok bluebeard's castle *simionato/petri*
turin **23 and 24 january 1953** rai torino orchestra and chorus	bach concerto for two violins/bach violin concerto 2/beethoven mass in c *orell/vinal/valletti/tozzi* *de vito and pelliccia, violins*
milan **4 march 1953** la scala orchestra and chorus	rossini l'italiana in algeri *dobbs/simionato/valletti/petri/bruscantini* *four further performances given*

milan
7 may 1953
la scala orchestra
and chorus

cilea adriana lecouvreur
rebaldi/dominguez/campora/poli/maionica
four further performances given

milan
1 june 1953
la scala orchestra
and chorus

monteverdi-ghedini l'incoronazione di poppea
petrella/canali/radev/gavarini/panerai/petri
three further performances given

scheveningen
19 june 1953
residentie orchestra

vivaldi le 4 stagioni/falla noches en los jardinos de espana/debussy la mer
henkemans, piano

aix
11, 16, 19 and 23
july 1953
paris conservatoire
orchestra and chorus

rossini il barbiere di siviglia
wilson/tangeman/valletti/capecchi/cortis

milan
29 and 30
july 1953
la scala orchestra

corelli six concerti from op 6

gardone
8 august 1953
la scala orchestra

vivaldi concerto op 3 no 11/pizetti suite per la pisanella/wagner tristan prelude and liebestod/beethoven symphony 6

stuttgart
18 october 1953
sdr orchestra

geminiani concerto op 3 no 2/ghedini pezzo concertante/pizzetti suite per la pisanella

milan
28 and 29
october 1953
la scala orchestra
and chorus

schubert symphony 5/ghedini l'olmeneta/beethoven mass in c
fineschi/dominguez/oncina/modesti

milan
31 october 1953
la scala orchestra

geminiani concerto op 3 no 2/schubert symphony 5/beethoven symphony 6

milan
7, 11, 13, 17,
20 and 23
december 1953
la scala orchestra
and chorus

catalani la wally
tebaldi/del monaco/guelfi

milan
28 january,
2, 8 and 11
february 1954
la scala orchestra
and chorus

bartok bluebeard's castle
dow/petri
stravinsky les noces
laszlo/elmo/berdini/sardi

milan
14, 18, 23 and
28 march and
3 april 1954
la scala orchestra
and chorus

rossini la cenerentola
simionato/gatta/cadoni/monti/bruscantini

milan
4, 6, 15 and 20
april 1954
la scala orchestra
and chorus

gluck alceste
callas/gavarini/zampieri/silveri/maionica

rome
23 april 1954
rai roma orchestra
and chorus

rossini il barbiere di siviglia
cadoni/monti/panerai/calabrese/cortis
first complete opera transmitted on italian television

florence
8, 11 and 13
may 1954
maggio musicale
orchestra and chorus

weber euryanthe
wilfert/borkh/vandenburg/kamann/a.welitsch

milan
8, 9, 10 and 14
june 1954
la scala orchestra

monteverdi il ballo delle ingrate
simionato/ballarini/ribacchi/arié

milan
18 and 19
june 1954
la scala orchestra

rossini signor bruschino overture/zafred concerto for string trio and orchestra/brahms symphony 4
trio di trieste, soloists

den haag
30 june 1954
residentie orchestra
la scala chorus

rossini la cenerentola
simionato/gatta/cadoni/valletti/bruscantini/petri

amsterdam
3 and 6 july 1954
residentie orchestra
la scala chorus

programme as for 30 june

scheveningen
7 july 1954
residentie orchestra

ravel ma mere l'oye/pijper piano concerto/
brahms symphony 4
bruins, piano

den haag
9 july 1954
residentie orchestra
la scala chorus

programme as for 30 june

cologne
27 september 1954
wdr orchestra

bonporti concerto op 11 no 8/brahms violin concerto/salviucci introduzione passacaglia e finale/falla el sombrero de 3 picos
de vito, violin

milan
11, 14, 19, 23 and 27 december 1954 and 1, 6 and 19 january 1955
la scala orchestra and chorus

donizetti l'elisir d'amore
carteri (ratti)/di stefano (monti)/panerai/tajo

milan
27 and 29 january and 2, 6 and 13 february 1955
la scala orchestra and chorus

weber der freischütz
de los angeles (pobbe)/ratti/picchi/rossi-lemeni/montarsolo/sordello

milan
3 and 6 march 1955
la scala orchestra and chorus

donizetti l'elisir d'amore
carteri/monti/sordello/tajo

venice
19 march 1955
la fenice orchestra

boccherini overture in d/salviucci introduzione passacaglia e finale/mussorgsky night on bare mountain/brahms symphony 4

florence
3 april 1955
maggio musicale orchestra and chorus

bonporti concerto op 11 no 8/ghedini l'olmeneto/cherubini requiem in c minor

florence
2, 4 and 8 may 1955
maggio musicale orchestra and chorus

donizetti don sebastiano
barbieri/poggi/mascherini/dondi/neri

milan
28 and 31 may
and 5 and 7
june 1955
la scala orchestra
and chorus

verdi la traviata
callas/di stefano (prandelli)/bastianini

den haag
24 june 1955
residentie orchestra
la scala chorus

rossini l'italiana in algeri
simionato/ratti/valletti/petri/cortis

amsterdam
26 and 28 june 1955
residentie orchestra
la scala chorus

programme as for 24 june

scheveningen
29 june 1955
residentie orchestra

bonporti concerto op 11 no 8/brahms piano concerto 2/salviucci introduzione passacaglia e finale/falla el sombrero de 3 picos
arrau, piano

amsterdam
30 june 1955
residentie orchestra

programme as for 29 june

amsterdam
5 july 1955
residenrie orchestra
la scala chorus

programme as for 24 june

edinburgh
23, 25, 27 and
29 august and
2 and 7
september 1955
royal philharmonic
glyndebourne chorus

verdi falstaff
rovere/cadoni/ratti/dominguez/oncina (miller)/corena/monachesi
these edinburgh festival performances were giulini's british début

milan
19 and 20
october 1955
la scala orchestra

haydn symphony 94/ghedini music for viola and strings/tchaikovsky symphony 2

chicago
3 and 8
november 1955
chicago symphony

vivaldi le 4 stagioni/pizzetti fedra overture/debussy la mer
giulini's american début

chicago
10 and 11
november 1955
chicago symphony

rossini italiana in algeri overture/haydn symphony 94/debussy la mer/ravel ma mere l'oye/falla el sombrero de 3 picos

florence
20 november 1955
maggio musicale orchestra

vivaldi le 4 stagioni/ghedini viola concerto/falla el sombrero de 3 picos
giuranna, viola

rome
18 december 1955
santa cecilia orchestra

haydn symphony 94/liszt piano concerto 2/pizzetti fedra overure/mussorgsky-ravel pictures at an exhibition
kempff, piano

rome
21 december 1955
santa cecilia orchestra

vivaldi le 4 stagioni/bartok bluebeard's castle
udovick/petri

milan
19, 23, 26 and
29 january and
2 and 5 february
1955
la scala orchestra and chorus

verdi la traviata
callas/raimondi/bastianin (protti)

milan
16 february 1956
la scala orchestra
and chorus

rossini il barbiere di siviglia
callas/canali/alva/gobbi/rossi-lemeni

milan
18 february 1956
la scala orchestra
and chorus

verdi la traviata
callas/raimondi/protti

milan
21 february 1956
la scala orchestra
and chorus

programme as for 16 february

milan
26 february 1956
la scala orchestra
and chorus

programme as for 18 february

vienna
28 and 29
february and
1 and 2 march 1956
vienna symphony

mozart divertimento 11/paganini violin concerto 1/
respighi fontane di roma/falla el sombrero de 3
picos
gimpel, violin

milan
3, 6, 15 and 18
march 1956
la scala orchestra
and chorus

rossini il barbiere di siviglia
callas (ratti)/canali/alva (monti)/gobbi/rossi-lemeni

florence
25 march 1956
maggio musicale
orchestra

mozart divertimento 11/haydn symphony 94/
brahms piano concerto 1
solomon, piano

milan
5 april 1956
la scala orchestra
and chorus

verdi la traviata
callas/raimondi/bastianini

venice
8 april 1956
la fenice orchestra

mozart divertimento 11/haydn symphony 94/
ravel ma mere l'oye/falla el sombrero de 3 picos

milan
14 april 1956
la scala orchestra
and chorus

performance as for 5 april

milan
16 april 1956
la scala orchestra
and chorus

rossini il barbiere di siviglia
de los angeles/canali/alva/gobbi/rossi-lemeni

milan
18 april 1956
la scala orchestra
and chorus

verdi la traviata
callas/raimondi/tagliabue

milan
20 april 1956
la scala orchestra
and chorus

performance as for 16 april

milan
21 april 1956
la scala orchestra
and chorus

verdi la traviata
callas/raimondi/bastianini

milan
22 april 1956
la scala orchestra
and chorus

performance as for 16 april

milan
25 and 27 april 1956
la scala orchestra
and chorus

performance as for 21 april

tel aviv
3 and 6 may 1956
israel philharmonic

haydn symphony 94/mozart sinfonia concertante for violin and viola/pizzetti fedra overture/mussorgsky-ravel pictures at an exhibition
grünschlag, violin and partos, viola

tel aviv
8 may 1956
israel philharmonic

rossini italiana in algeri overture/saint-saens cello concerto 1/mussorgsky night on bare mountain/mussorgsky-ravel pictures at an exhibition
tortelier, cello

haifa
10 may 1956
israel philharmonic

rossini la cenerentola overture/saint-saens cello 1/pizzetti fedra overture/mussorgsky-ravel pictures at an exhibtion
tortelier, cello

tel aviv
12 may 1956
israel philharmonic

performance as for 8 may

tel aviv
13 and 14 may 1956
israel philharmonic

haydn symphony 94/brahms double concerto/pizzetti fedra overture/mussorgsky-ravel pictures at an exhibition
polishuk, violin and ginsburg, cello

jerusalem
17 may 1956
israel philharmonic

performance as for 3 may

tel aviv
20 may 1956
israel philharmonic

performance as for 13 and 14 may

tel aviv
21 may 1956
israel philharmonic

rossini italiana in algeri overture/haydn symphony 94/mussorgsky night on bare mountain/mussorgsky-ravel pictures at an exhibition

haifa
23 may 1956
israel philharmonic

programme as for 13 and 14 may

tel aviv
26 may 1956
israel philharmonic

prokofiev love of 3 oranges suite/rossini italiana in algeri overture/haydn symphony 94/brahms symphony 2

tel aviv
28 may 1956
israel philharmonic

programme as for 13 and 14 may

tel aviv
29 may 1956
israel philharmonic

haydn symphony 94/hoffmeister viola concerto/ mussorgsky-ravel pictures at an exhibition
benyamini, viola

tel aviv
30 may 1956
israel philharmonic

programme as for 13 and 14 may

den haag
29 june 1956
residentie orchestra
la scala chorus

verdi falstaff
broggini/cadoni/ratti/palombini/oncina/corena/ monachesi

amsterdam
1 and 3 july 1956
residentie orchestra
la scala chorus

programme as for 29 june

den haag
5 july 1956
residentie orchestra
la scala chorus

programme as for 29 june

rotterdam
7 july 1956
residentie orchestra
la scala chorus

programme as for 29 june

amsterdam
10 july 1956
residentie orchestra
la scala chorus

programme as for 29 june

aix
25 and 28 july and
1 august 1956
paris conservatoire
orchestra and chorus

rossini il barbiere di siviglia
ratti/ cadoni/ oncina/ panerai/ arié

milan
15, 16 and 17
october 1956
la scala orchestra

salviucci introduzione passacaglia e finale/mozart concerto for 2 pianos/beethoven symphony 6
gorini and lorenzi, pianos

florence
13 and 15
january 1957
maggio musicale
orchestra and chorus

weber der freischütz
wilfert/ steffek/ feiersinger/ gynrod/ stern/ hofmann

florence
24 february 1957
maggio musicale
orchestra

schumann programme
manfred overture/cello concerto/symphony 3
mainardi, cello

vienna
3, 4 and 5
april 1957
vienna symphony

ravel ma mere l'oye/mendelssohn violin concerto/ boccherini symphony in c/stravinsky firebird suite
martzy, violin

florence
9, 12 and 15
may 1957
maggio musicale
orchestra and chorus

cherubini les abencérages
cerquetti/misciano/roney/petri

turin
21 may 1957
rai torino orchestra

boccherini symphony in c/debussy jeux/
mussorgsky-ravel pictures at an exhibition

turin
24 may 1957
rai torino orchestra

brahms programme
tragic overture/piano concerto 1/symphony 1
serkin, piano

vienna
29 and 30 may 1957
vienna symphony

rossini barbiere di siviglia overture/mussorgsky-
ravel pictures at an exhibition/brahms
symphony 2

milan
6 and 7 june 1957
la scala orchestra

schumann symphony 3/zafred viola concerto/
stravinsky firebird suite
giuranna, viola

scheveningen
15 and 17 june 1957
residentie orchestra
holland festival chorus

verdi messa da requiem
brouwenstijn/pirazzini/misciano/arié

rotterdam
18 june 1957
residentie orchestra
holland festival chorus

programme as for 15 and 17 june

amsterdam
20 june 1957
residentie orchestra
holland festival chorus

programme as for 15 and 17 june

lucerne
21 august 1957
swiss festival orchestra

boccherini symphony in c/schumann piano concerto/
ravel ma mere l'oye/falla el sombrero de 3 picos
anda, piano

cologne
7 october 1957
wdr orchestra

ghedini pezzo concertante/haydn cello concerto 2/ brahms symphony 4
borwitzky, cello

vienna
11, 12 and 13 october 1957
vienna symphony

wolf-ferrari 4 rusteghi and segreto di susanna intermezzi/ravel piano concerto in g/tchaikovsky symphony 6
santoliquido, piano

amsterdam
30 and 31 october 1957
concertgebouw orchestra

boccherini symphony in c/badings concerto for 2 violins/mussorgsky ravel pictures at an exhibition
olof and krebbers, violins

den haag
2 november 1957
concertgebouw orchestra

geminiani concerto op 3 no 2/mozart piano concerto 25/turchi piccolo concerto notturno/ falla el sombrero de 3 picos
scarpini, piano

amsterdam
3 november 1957
concertgebouw orchestra

programme as for 2 november

rotterdam
5 november 1957
concertgebouw orchestra

programme as for 30 and 31 october

amsterdam
6 and 7 november 1957
concertgebouw orchestra

haydn symphony 94/salviucci introduzione passacaglia e finale/tchaikovsky symphony 2

amsterdam
9 and 10
november 1957
concertgebouw
orchestra

boccherini symphony in c/mozart piano concerto 25/mussorgsky-ravel pictures at an exhibition
scarpini, piano

venice
8 and 9
december 1957
la fenice orchestra
and chorus

verdi messa da requiem
ligabue/ minarchi (cossotto)/ misciano/ cava (vinco)

rome
15 december 1957
santa cecilia orchestra
and chorus

beethoven symphony 6/cherubini requiem in c minor

rome
18 december 1957
santa cecilia orchestra

brahms tragic overture/lalo symphonie espagnole/ schumann symphony 3
gimpel, violin

chicago
14 january 1958
chicago symphony

bonporti concerto op 11 no 8/debussy jeux/ stravinsky firebird suite/beethoven symphony 5

chicago
16 and 17
january 1958
chicago symphony

mussorgsky khovantschina prelude/dvorak symphony 8/brahms symphony 4

milwaukee
20 january 1958
chicago symphony

bonporti concerto op 11 no 8/beethoven piano concerto 3/brahms symphony 4
janis, piano

chicago
23 and 24
january 1958
chicago symphony

boccherini symphony in c minor/ghedini pezzo concertante/tchaikovsky symphony 2

chicago
28 january 1958
chicago symphony

mozart symphony 35/respighi fontane di roma/
brahms symphony 4

chicago
30 and 31
january 1958
chicago symphony

schumann symphony 3/wolf-ferrari segreto di
susanna overture/turchi piccolo concerto
notturno/ravel daphnis et chloé second suite

chicago
1 february 1958
chicago symphony

wolf-ferrari segreto di susanna overture/
tchaikovsky symphony 2/brahms piano concerto 1
fleisher, piano

milwaukee
3 february 1958
chicago symphony

boccherini symphony in c minor/ghedini pezzo
concertante/tchaikovsky symphony 2

florence
20 february 1958
maggio musicale
orchestra

beethoven symphony 6/ghedini pezzo concertante/
ravel daphnis et chloé second suite

florence
23 february 1958
maggio musicale
orchestra

wolf-ferrari 4 rusteghi and segreto di susanna
overtures/dvorak symphony 8/brahms symphony 1

tel aviv
16, 17 and 19
march 1958
israel philharmonic
tel aviv chorus

rossini il barbiere di siviglia
berganza/ samsonov/ spina/ monachesi/ arié
these were probably concert performances of the opera

haifa
20 march 1958
israel philharmonic
tel aviv chorus

programme as for 16, 17 and 19 march

113

tel aviv
22, 24 and 25
march 1958
israel philharmonic
tel aviv chorus

programme as for 16, 17 and 19 march

jerusalem
27 march 1958
israel philharmonic
tel aviv chorus

programme as for 16, 17 and 19 march

tel aviv
29 march 1958
israel philharmonic

programme of operatic overtures and arias by
rossini and verdi
berganza/spina/monachesi/cortis/arié

tel aviv
31 march 1958
israel philharmonic
tel aviv chorus

programme as for 16, 17 and 19 march

tel aviv
1 april 1958
israel philharmonic

rossini italiana in algeri overture/pergolesi la serva
padrona/brahms symphony 2
menotti/cortis

haifa
2 and 3 april 1958
israel philharmonic

programme as for 1 april

tel aviv
6 and 7 april 1958
israel philharmonic

programme as for 1 april

netanya
8 april 1958
israel philharmonic

rossini barbiere di siviglia overture/beethoven
piano concerto 3/brahms symphony 2
salzman, piano

haifa
9 april 1958
israel philharmonic

programme as for 1 april

tel aviv
13 april 1958
israel philharmonic

programme as for 1 april

jerusalem
14 april 1958
israel philharmonic

programme as for 1 april

london
9, 12 and 15
may 1958
covent garden
orchestra and chorus

verdi don carlo
brouwenstijn/barbieri/vickers/gobbi/christoff/stefanoni

london
16 may 1958
philharmonia

brahms programme
tragic overture/piano concerto 2/symphony 1
richter-haaser, piano

london
19, 21, 24, 26 and
28 may 1958
covent garden
orchestra and chorus

programme as for 9, 12 and 15 may

brussels
22 june 1958
la scala orchestra

brahms symphony 4/pizzetti fedra overture/
mussorgsky-ravel pictures at an exhibition

scheveningen
2 july 1958
residentie orchestra

vivaldi le 4 stagioni/mussorgsky night on bare
mountain/stravinsky firebird suite
olof, violin

amsterdam
4 july 1958
residentie orchestra

programme as for 2 july

aix
21, 26 and 30
july 1958
paris conservatoire
orchestra and chorus

rossini il barbiere di siviglia
berganza/betti/spina/panerai/calabrese

stockholm
19 october 1958
swedish radio orchestra

mozart programme
divertimento 11/sinfonia concertante for violin
and viola/mia speranza adorata/symphony 39
hallin/nilsson, violin and appelbom, viola

london
27 october 1958
philharmonia

beethoven programme
egmont overture/symphony 6/symphony 5

cologne
3 november 1958
wdr orchestra

turchi piccolo concerto notturno/schumann
cello concerto/dvorak symphony 8
janigro, cello

milan
12 and 13
november 1958
la scala orchestra

brahms programme
tragic overture/double concerto/symphony 1
de vito, violin and baldovino, cello

florence
7 december 1958
maggio musicale
orchestra

turchi piccolo concerto notturno/bartok rhapsody
for piano and orchestra/beethoven symphony 5
foldes, piano

venice
9 december 1958
la fenice orchestra
and chorus

verdi messa da requiem
ligabue/cossotto/misciano/vinco

tel aviv
3, 11 and 12
january 1959
israel philharmonic
tel aviv chorus

verdi messa da requiem
angioletti/carturan/zampieri/arié

haifa
14 january 1959
israel philharmonic
tel aviv chorus

programme as for 3, 11 and 12 january

jerusalem
15 january 1959
israel philharmonic
tel aviv chorus

ptogramme as for 3, 11 and 12 january

tel aviv
17 and 19
january 1959
israel philharmonic
tel aviv chorus

programme as for 3, 11 and 12 january

haifa
21 and 22
january 1959
israel philharmonic
tel aviv chorus

programme as for 3, 11 and 12 january

tel aviv
24 and 25
january 1959
israel philharmonic
tel aviv chorus

programme as for 3, 11 and 12 january

tel aviv
7, 9, 11, 12, 14, 16,
18, 19, 21, 23, 24 and
26 february 1959
israel philharmonic
renat chorus

verdi falstaff
ligabue/ cadoni/ adani/ dominguez/ spina/ corena/ monachesi

milan
3 april 1959
la scala orchestra

falla el sombrero de 3 picos/peragallo violin
concerto/dvorak symphony 8
gulli, violin

london
12 april 1959
philharmonia

brahms programme
piano concerto 1/symphony 1
ts'ong, piano

london
22, 24 and 28
april and
1 and 4 may 1959
covent garden
orchestra and chorus

verdi don carlo
brouwenstijn/hoffman/vickers/evans/christoff/stefanoni

london
7 june 1959
philharmonia

tchaikovsky symphony 6/chopin piano concerto 2/
stravinsky firebird suite
haskil, piano

london
11 june 1959
philharmonia

rossini italiana in algeri overture/franck variations
symphoniques/wagner tristan prelude and
liebestod/liszt hungarian fantasia/mussorgsky-
ravel pictures at an exhibition
cziffra, piano

den haag
24 june 1959
netherlands chamber
and utrecht
municipal orchestras
holland festival chorus

haydn il mondo della luna
adani/rizzoli/casoni/alva/pedani/cortis
performances to commemorate 150 th anniversary of the
composer's death

amsterdam
27 june 1959
netherlands chamber
and utrecht
municipal orchestras
holland festival chorus

programme as for 24 june

118
rotterdam *programme as for 24 june*
30 june 1959
netherlands chamber
and utrecht
municipal orchestras
holland festival chorus

den haag *programme as for 24 june*
3 july 1959
netherlands chamber
and utrecht
municipal orchestras
holland fesrival chorus

utrecht *programme as for 24 june*
6 july 1959
netherlands chamber
and utrecht
municipal orchestras
holland festival chorus

scheveningen *mozart programme*
8 july 1959 symphony 35/concert arias/divertimento 11/
residentie orchestra symphony 39
 stader

amsterdam *programme as for 24 june*
10 july 1959
netherlands chamber
and utrecht
municipal orchestras
holland festival chorus

aix *programme as for 24 june*
18, 21, 25 and
29 july 1959
netherlands chamber
and utrecht
municipal orchestras
holland festival chorus

lucerne **19 august 1959** swiss festival orchestra	brahms tragic overture/dvorak violin concerto/ pizzetti fedra overture/mussorgsky-ravel pictures at an exhibition *milstein, violin*
london **28 september 1959** philharmonia orchestra and chorus	mozart le nozze di figaro *schwarzkopf/moffo/cossotto/taddei/wächter* *this was a concert performance in conjunction with* *columbia recording sessions*
den haag **31 october 1959** concertgebouw orchestra	locatelli concerto grosso 8/malipiero symphony 4/ tchaikovsky symphony 2
amsterdam **1 november 1959** concertgebouw orchestra	*programme as for 31 october*
amsterdam **4 and 5** **november 1959** concertgebouw orchestra	malipiero symphony 4/ravel ma mere l'oye/brahms symphony 4
amsterdam **7 and 8** **november 1959** concertgebouw orchestra	mozart piano concerto 6/ravel ma mere l'oye/ henkemans passacaglia and gigue/schumann symphony 3 *henkemans, piano*
arnhem **10 november 1959** concertgebouw orchestra	*programme as for 4 and 5 november*
amsterdam **11 and 12** **november 1959** concertgebouw orchestra	haydn symphony 44/vivaldi viola concerto in a/ hindemith kammermusik 6/tchaikovsky symphony 2 *giuranna, viola*

florence
6 december 1959
maggio musicale
orchestra

mozart symphony 39/zafred harp concerto/brahms symphony 2
aldovandri, harp

tel aviv
13, 15, 17, 18, 20, 22, 24, 25, 27 and 29 february and 2, 3, 5, 7, 8 and 10 march 1960
israel philharmonic
renat chorus

mozart le nozze di figaro
ligabue/adani/malagu/tadeo/pedani

vienna
15, 16 and 17 march 1960
vienna symphony

respighi ancient airs and dances suite 3/chopin piano concerto 2/brahms symphony 1
haskil, piano

frankfurt
25 march 1960
orchestra of
hessischer rundfunk

mendelssohn violin concerto/malipiero symphony 4
grumiaux, violin

stockholm
10 april 1960
swedish radio
orchestra and chorus

respighi ancient airs and dances suite 3/boccherini symphony in c minor/rossini italiana in algeri overture/vivaldi gloria
c.nilsson/nygren-almquist/ericson

london
25 april 1960
philharmonia

verdi vespri siciliani overture/rachmaninov paganini rhapsody/dvorak symphony 8/falla sombrero de 3 picos
a.tchaikovsky, piano

london
28 april 1960
philharmonia

mozart symphony 39/strauss 4 letzte lieder/schubert symphony 8/ravel daphnis et chloé second suite
schwarzkopf

london
**16, 19, 21, 23, 25
and 27 may 1960**
covent garden
orchestra and chorus

vienna
30 may 1960
philharmonia

london
**31 may and
2 june 1960**
covent garden
orchestra and chorus

vienna
9 june 1960
philharmonia
orchestra and chorus

london
12 june 1960
philharmonia
orchestra and chorus

amsterdam
22 june 1960
concertgebouw
orchestra
groot omroep chorus

utrecht
23 june 1960
concertgebouw
orchestra
groot omroep chorus

rossini il barbiere di siviglia
berganza/veasey/alva/panerai/vinco

mozart symphony 39/4 letzte lieder/wagner tristan
prelude and liebestod/stravinsky firebird suite
schwarzkopf

programme as for 16, 19, 21, 23, 25 and 27 may

verdi messa da requiem
l.price/cossotto/ottolini/vinco

verdi messa da requiem
sutherland/cossotto/ottoloni/vinco

bonporti concerto op 11 no 8/vivaldi gloria/
verdi 4 pezzi sacri
schwarzkopf/boese

programme as for 22 june

scheveningen
24 june 1960
concertgebouw
orchestra
groot omroep chorus

programme as for 22 june

scheveningen
2 july 1960
netherlands
chamber orchestra

vivaldi viola concerto in a/respighi ancient airs and
dances suite 3/mozart ch'io mi scordi di te/mozart
arias from cosi fan tutte/haydn symphony 94
schwarzkopf/curzio, piano and nijland, viola

rotterdam
3 july 1960
netherlands
chamber orchestra

programme as for 2 july

amsterdam
5 july 1960
netherlands
chamber orchestra

programme as for 2 july

edinburgh
21 august 1960
philharmonia
orchestra and chorus

verdi messa da requiem
sutherland/cossotto/ottolini/vinco

edinburgh
24 august 1960
philharmonia

mozart symphony 39/beethoven piano concerto 1/
brahms symphony 1
arrau, piano

lucerne
3 september 1960
philharmonia

rossini italiana in algeri overture/dvorak symphony 8/
schumann piano concerto/wagner tristan prelude
and liebestod
a.fischer, piano

tel aviv
18 and 20
september 1960
israel philharmonic

haydn symphony 94/sheriff shir hamaalot/
stravinsky firebird suite/brahms symphony 4

tel aviv
25 and 26
september 1960
israel philharmonic

weber freischütz overture/ben-haim capriccio for
piano and orchestra/stravinsky firebird suite/
brahms symphony 4
salzman, piano

tel aviv
27 september 1960
israel philharmonic

beethoven symphony 6/respighi ancient airs and
dances suite 3/falla el sombrero de 3 picos

haifa
28 and 29
september 1960
israel philharmonic

beethoven symphony 6/respighi ancient airs and
dances suite 3/sheriff shir hamaalot/stravinsky
firebird suite

jerusalem
2 october 1960
israel philharmonic

programme as for 25 and 26 september

haifa
4 october 1960
israel philharmonic

weber freischütz overture/ben-haim capriccio for
piano and orchestra/falla el sombrero de 3 picos/
brahms symphony 4
salzman, piano

tel aviv
6 october 1960
israel philharmonic

beethoven symphony 6/respighi ancient airs and
dances suite 3/ben-haim capriccio for piano and
orchestra/falla el sombrero de 3 picos
salzman, piano

tel aviv
8 october 1960
israel philharmonic

weber freischütz overture/sheriff shir hamaalot/
stravinsky firebird suite/brahms symphony 4

world tour by israel philharmonic orchestra

paris
10 october 1960
israel philharmonic

brahms symphony 4/respighi ancient airs and dances suite 3/sheriff shir hamaalot/falla el sombrero de 3 picos

paris
11 october 1960
israel philharmonic

beethoven symphony 6/weber freischütz overture/ben-haim capriccio for piano and orchestra/stravinsky firebird suite
salzman, piano

long island
15 october 1960
israel philharmonic

weber freischütz overture/sheriff shir hamaalot/stravinsky firebird suite/brahms symphony 1

new york
16 october 1960
israel philharmonic

programme as for 15 october

new york
18 october 1960
israel philharmonic

beethoven symphony 6/respighi ancient airs and dances suite 3/ben-haim capriccio for piano and orchestra/falla el sombrero de 3 picos
salzman, piano

baltimore
20 october 1960
israel philharmonic

weber freischütz overture/sheriff shir hamaalot/stravinsky firebird suite/brahms symphony 4

washington
22 october 1960
israel philharmonic

programme as for 20 october

newark
23 october 1960
israel philharmonic

weber freischütz overture/ben-haim capriccio for piano and orchestra/stravinsky firebird suite/brahms symphony 4
salzman, piano

hartford
24 october 1960
israel philharmonic

brahms symphony 4/respighi ancient airs and dances suite 3/ben-haim capriccio for piano and orchestra/falla el sombrero de 3 picos
salzman, piano

new haven
25 october 1960
israel philharmonic

programme as for 18 october

new london
26 october 1960
israel philharmonic

weber freischütz overture/haydn symphony 94/ sheriff shir hamaalot/brahms symphony 1

rochester
29 october 1960
israel philharmonic

programme as for 22 october

chicago
31 october 1960
israel philharmonic

mendelssohn violin concerto/falla el sombreo de 3 picos
stern, violin

milwaukee
3 november 1960
israel philharmonic

programme as for 20 october

toronto
7 november 1960
israel philharmonic

weber freischütz overture/ben-haim capriccio for piano and orchestra/stravinsky firebird suite/ brahms symphony 1
salzman, piano

montreal
8 november 1960
israel philharmonic

programme as for 23 october

burlington
9 november 1960
israel philharmonic

weber freischütz overture/haydn symphony 94/ dvorak symphony 8

providence
10 november 1960
israel philharmonic

programme as for 23 october

126
buffalo　　　　　　　　　*programme as for 24 october*
13 november 1960
israel philharmonic

minneapolis　　　　　　　*programme as for 22 october*
14 november 1960
israel philhrmonic

san francisco　　　　　　*programme as for 22 october*
17 november 1960
israel philharmonic

berkeley　　　　　　　　dvorak symphony 8/respighi ancient airs and dances
19 november 1960　　　　suite 3/ben-haim capriccio for piano and orchestra/
israel philharmonic　　　　　falla el sombrero de 3 picos
　　　　　　　　　　　　　　salzman, piano

los angeles　　　　　　　*programme as for 16 october*
20 november 1960
israel philharmonic

san diego　　　　　　　　*programme as for 23 october*
21 november 1960
israel philharmonic

mexico city　　　　　　　*programme as for 22 october*
22 november 1960
israel philharmonic

mexico city　　　　　　　*programme as foe 19 november*
23 november 1960
israel philharmonic

mexico city　　　　　　　haydn symphony 94/schumann piano concerto/
24 november 1960　　　　beethoven symphony 5
israel philharmonic　　　　　*salzman, piano*

chicago
26 november 1960
israel philharmonic

programme as for 17 november

philadelphia
27 november 1960
israel philharmonic

weber freischütz overture/mozart nozze di figaro
overture/mozart arias/stravinsky firebird suite/
brahms symphony 1
peters

tokyo
5 december 1960
israel philharmonic

programme as for 8 october

tokyo
6 december 1960
israel philharmonic

programme as for 25 october

osaka
8 december 1960
israel philharmonic

verdi forza de destino overture/dvorak symphony 8/
beethoven symphony 5

osaka
10 december 1960
israel philharmonic

programme as for 25 october

okayama
11 december 1960
israel philharmonic

programme as for 8 december

kyoto
13 december 1960
israel philharmonic

programme as for 8 october

nagoya
14 december 1960
israel philharmonic

programme as for 6 october

yokohama
15 december 1960
israel philharmonic

programme as for 6 october

tokyo　　　　　　　　　*programme as for 8 december*
18 december 1960
israel philharmonic

new delhi　　　　　　　*programme as for 8 october*
20 december 1960
israel philharmonic

bombay　　　　　　　　*programme as for 8 october*
21 december 1960
israel philharmonic
end of world tour by israel philharmonic orchestra

london　　　　　　　　verdi messa da requiem
22 january 1961　　　　*shuard/ludwig/ottolini/zaccaria*
philharmonia
orchestra and chorus

london　　　　　　　　mozart le nozze di figaro
6 february 1961　　　　*schwarzkopf/söderström/berganza/corena/blanc*
philharmonia　　　　　　　*this was a concert performance of the opera*
orchestra and chorus

london　　　　　　　　mozart don giovanni
20 february 1961　　　*schwarzkopf/grümmer/freni/haefliger/wächter/frick*
philharmonia　　　　　　　*this was a concert performance of the opera*
orchestra and chorus

florence　　　　　　　　*brahms programme*
26 february 1961　　　tragic overture/piano concerto 1/symphony 4
maggio musicale　　　　　*perticaroli, piano*
orchestra

turin　　　　　　　　　beethoven egmont overture/lalo cello concerto/
24 march 1961　　　　schumann symphony 3
rai torino orchestra　　　　*fournier, cello*

florence
31 march 1961
maggio musicale
orchestra

weber freischütz overture/ghedini divertimento for violin and orchestra/schumann symphony 3
luzzato, violin

rome
9 april 1961
santa cecilia
orchestra and chorus

vivaldi-casella concerto in c/fauré requiem/beethoven piano concerto 5
panni/candia/santoliquido, piano

rome
12 april 1961
santa cecilia orchestra

boccherini symphony in c minor/tchaikovsky piano concerto 1/schumann symphony 3
gilels, piano

london
10 and 12 may 1961
covent garden
orchestra and chorus

verdi falstaff
angioletti/veasey/freni/resnik/alva/evans/shaw

london
16 may 1961
philharmonia

verdi forza del destino overture/chopin piano concerto 2/tchaikovsky piano concerto 1/mussorgsky-ravel pictures at an exhibition
rubinstein, piano

london
17, 20, 22, 25 and 27 may 1961
covent garden
orchestra and chorus

programme as for 10 and 12 may

den haag
19 june 1961
residentie orchestra
holland festival chorus

mozart le nozze di figaro
schwarzkopf/sciutti/malagu/taddei/prey

amsterdam
23 june 1961
residentie orchestra
holland festival chorus

programme as for 19 june

utrecht *programme as for 19 june*
26 june 1961
residentie orchestra
holland festival chorus

amsterdam geminiani concerto grosso 12/boccherini symphony/
27 june 1961 handel arias from rinaldo, giulio cesare and messiah/
netherlands mozart divertimento 15
chamber orchestra *berganza*

den haag *programme as for 19 june*
29 june 1961
residentie orchestra
holland festival chorus

scheveningen *programme as for 27 june*
1 july 1961
netherlands
chamber orchestra

amsterdam mozart le nozze di figaro
3 july 1961 *watson/tyler (sciutti)/berganza/taddei/prey*
residentie orchestra
holland festival chorus

rotterdam *programme as for 3 july*
6 july 1961
residentie orchestra
holland festival chorus

amsterdam *programme as for 3 july*
9 july 1961
residentie orchestra
holland festival chorus

den haag *programme as for 3 july*
13 july 1961
residentie orchestra
holland festival chorus

edinburgh
31 august and 2
and 5 september 1961
covent garden
orchestra and chorus

rossini il barbiere di siviglia
casoni/veasey/alva/panerai/christoff

edinburgh
7 september 1961
philharmonia

tchaikovsky symphony 6/mussorgsky khovantschina
prelude/mussorgsky-ravel pictures at an exhibition

edinburgh
8 september 1961
covent garden
orchestra and chorus

programme as for 31 august and 2 and 5 september

edinburgh
9 september 1961
philharmonia

mozart symphony 35/mozart sinfonia concertante
for violin and viola/britten serenade for tenor,
horn and strings/britten young person's guide
pears/goldberg, violin/giuranna, viola/civil, horn

leeds
12 october 1961
philharmonia
leeds festival chorus

verdi messa da requiem
cavalli/gorr/misciano/trama

leeds
13 october 1961
philharmonia
leeds festival chorus

vivaldi concerto for 2 violins/vivaldi gloria/
stravinsky les noces
simon/watts/galliver/cameron

leeds
14 october 1961
philharmonia
leeds festival chorus

programme as for 12 october

den haag
28 and 29
october 1961
concertgebouw
orchestra

haydn symphony 104/ravel shéhérazade/ravel-
rosenthal 5 greek folksongs/falla el amor brujo/
falla el sombrero de 3 picos
kolassi

amsterdam
1 and 2 november 1961
concertgebouw
orchestra

programme as for 28 and 29 october

amsterdam
4 and 5 november 1961
concertgebouw
orchestra

ghedini sonata da camera/liszt piano concerto 1/
beethoven symphony 6
bar-jilan, piano

tel aviv
2, 4, 6, 7, 9, 11
13, 14, 16 and
18 december 1961
israel philharmonic
renat chorus

rossini l'italiana in algeri
berganza/alva/montarsolo/bruscantini

jerusalem
20 and 21
december 1961
israel philharmonic
renat chorus

programme as for 2 december

london
16 january 1962
philharmonia

falla programme
harpsichord concerto/excerpts from la vida breve/
el amor brujo/el sombrero de 3 picos
berganza/malcolm, harpsichord

london
21 january 1962
philharmonia
orchestra and chorus

verdi messa da requiem
ross/gorr/gedda/ghiaurov

chicago
15 and 16
february 1962
chicago symphony
orchestra and chorus

brahms symphony 1/verdi 4 pezzi sacri

milwaukee
19 february 1962
chicago symphony

britten young person's guide/wagner tristan
prelude and liebestod/brahms symphony 1

chicago
22, 23 and 24
february 1962
chicago symphony

haydn symphony 104/prokofiev violin concerto 1/
britten young person's guide/wagner tristan
prelude and liebestod
milstein, violin

boston
2, 3, 4 and
6 march 1962
boston symphony
harvard and
radcliffe choruses

rossini italiana in algeri overture/ghedini sonata
da camera/tchaikovsky symphony 2/verdi 4 pezzi
sacri

boston
9 and 10 march 1962
boston symphony

haydn symphony 94/britten young person's guide/
dvorak symphony 9

florence
25 march 1962
maggio musicale
orchestra and chorus

vivaldi gloria/falla el amor brujo/ravel rapsodie
espagnole
fioironi/londi/pellegrini

vienna
4 and 5 april 1962
vienna symphony

franck symphony in d minor/prokofiev violin
concerto 1/ravel rapsodie espagnole
wilkomirska, violin

london
16 april 1962
philharmonia

bach concerto for 4 harpsichords/britten young
person's guide/stravinsky octet/ravel rapsodie
espagnole
tunnard/malcolm/slater/keys

london
24 april 1962
philharmonia

weber freischütz overture/brahms symphony 4/
sibelius violin concerto/debussy la mer
szeryng, violin

london
30 april 1962
philharmonia
orchestra and chorus

fauré requiem/verdi 4 pezzi sacri
baker/souzay

turin
18 may 1962
rai torino orchestra
and chorus

beethoven egmont overture/pizzetti cello concerto/
verdi 4 pezzi sacri
mainardi, cello

milan
8 and 9 june 1962
philharmonia

brahms symphony 1/britten young person's guide/
mussorgsky-ravel pictures at an exhibition

den haag
19 june 1962
residentie orchestra
holland festival chorus

rossini il barbiere di siviglia
berganza/tyler/alva/capecchi/trama

rotterdam
21 june 1962
residentie orchestra
holland festival chorus

programme as for 19 june

amsterdam
23 june 1962
residentie orchestra
holland festival chorus

programme as for 19 june

utrecht
25 june 1962
residentie orchestra
holland festival chorus

programme as for 19 june

den haag
28 june 1962
residentie orchestra
holland festival chorus

programme as for 19 june

edinburgh
6 september 1962
philharmonia

rossini guglielmo tell overture/dvorak cello concerto/brahms symphony 1
rostropovich, cello

edinburgh
8 september 1962
philharmonia

beethoven symphony 6/britten 4 sea interludes/debussy la mer

london
7 october 1962
philharmonia
orchestra and chorus

mozart eine kleine nachtmusik/serenade for tenor, horn and strings/debussy nuages et fetes/verdi 4 pezzi sacri
baker/pears/civil, horn

london
20 october 1962
philharmonia

brahms programme
haydn variations/violin concerto/symphony 4
milstein, violin

london
5 november 1962
philharmonia

brahms programme
tragic overture/piano concerto 1/piano concerto 2
rubinstein, piano

london
11 november 1962
philharmonia

brahms programme
symphony 2/symphony 1

florence
7 february 1963
maggio musicale
orchestra and chorus

beethoven symphony 3/debussy 3 nocturnes/verdi forza del destino overture

tel aviv
30 april and
1, 2 and 4 may 1963
israel philharmonic

haydn symphony 104/prokofiev violin concerto 1/falla el amor brujo/ravel daphnis et chloé second suite/verdi forza del destino overture
milstein, violin

tel aviv
5 may 1963
israel philharmonic

haydn symphony 104/brahms violin concerto/falla el amor brujo/ravel daphnis et chloé second suite/verdi forza del destino overture
milstein, violin

haifa
7 and 8 may 1963
israel philharmonic

programme as for 5 may

haifa
9 may 1963
israel philharmonic

programme as for 30 april

tel aviv
11 may 1963
israel philharmonic

programme as for 5 may

jerusalem
12 may 1963
israel philharmonic

haydn symphony 104/prokofiev violin concerto 1/
falla el amor brujo/verdi forza del destino overture
milstein, violin

tel aviv
13 may 1963
israel philharmonic

programme as for 5 may

den haag
20 june 1963
concertgebouw
orchestra
holland festival chorus

verdi falstaff
ligabue/cadoni/freni/barbieri/alva/corena/capecchi

london
23 june 1963
philharmonia
orchestra and chorus

verdi messa da requiem
schwarzkopf/ludwig/gedda/ghiaurov

amsterdam
25 june 1963
concertgebouw
orchestra
holland festival chorus

programme as for 20 june

rotterdam
27 june 1963
concertgebouw
orchestra
holland festival chorus

programme as for 20 june

amsterdam
30 june 1963
concertgebouw
orchestra members

gounod petite symphonie/stravinsky octet/
mozart serenade for 13 wind

amsterdam
2 july 1963
concertgebouw
orchestra
holland festival chorus

programme as for 20 june

den haag
6 july 1963
concertgebouw
orchestra
holland festival chorus

programme as for 20 june

amsterdam
10 july 1963
concertgebouw
orchestra
holland festival chorus

programme as for 20 june

london
5 august 1963
philharmonia
orchestra and chorus

verdi messa da requiem
shuard/reynolds/lewis/ward

london
8 august 1963
philharmonia

verdi vespri siciliani overture/brahms violin concerto/
dvorak symphony 8/falla el sombrero de 3 picos
gotkovsky, violin

stesa
5 september 1963
philharmonia

rossini guglielmo tell overture/schubert symphony 8/
brahms symphony 4

lucerne
10 september 1963
philharmonia

verdi vespri siciliani overture/tchaikovsky violin concerto/falla el amor brujo/ravel rapsodie espagnole
rubio/ milstein, violin

concerts in parma to celebrate 150 th anniversary of verdi's birth

parma
5 october 1963
philharmonia
orchestra and chorus

verdi programme
choruses from nabucco and i lombardi/vespri siciliani overture/4 pezzi sacri

parma
6 october 1963
philharmonia
orchestra and chorus

verdi messa da requiem
maragliano/ dominguez/ labo/ arié

florence
7 october 1963
philharmonia

verdi vespri siciliani overture/beethoven symphony 7/brahms symphony 4

budapest
24 october 1963
hungarian state
symphony orchestra

beethoven egmont overture/beethoven symphony 6/ mussorgsky-ravel pictures at an exhibition

budapest
28 october 1963
hungarian state
symphony orchestra
and chorus

verdi 4 pezzi sacri/brahms symphony 1

venice
10 november 1963
la fenice orchestra
and chorus

beethoven programme
symphony 8/symphony 9
kalmus/ malagu/ casellato-lamberti/ trama

cologne **21 november 1963** wdr orchestra	beethoven symphony 7/malipiero cello concerto/ravel rapsodie espagnole *palm, cello*
london **25 november 1963** philharmonia	boccherini symphony in c minor/mozart piano concerto 20/grieg piano concerto/rossini semiramide overture *rubinstein, piano*
rome **26 december 1963** rome opera orchestra and chorus	verdi falstaff *ligabue (londi)/cadoni/adani (freni)/batbieri/alva (bottazzo)/gobbi/capecchi* *4 further performances given*
tel aviv **20, 23, 25 and** **27 january 1964** israel philharmonic renat chorus	mozart don giovanni *londi/lorengar/corenne/bottazzo/capecchi/monachesi/ferrin*
haifa **28 and 29** **january 1964** israel philharmonic	mozart divertimento 11/arias from cosi fan tutte and le nozze di figaro/beethoven symphony 7 *lorengar*
tel aviv **30 january and** **1, 3 and 5** **february 1964** israel philharmonic renat chorus	*programme as for 20 january*
haifa **6 february 1964** israel philharmonic	*programme as for 28 and 29 january*
tel aviv **8, 9, 11, 13, 15, 16** **and 18 february 1964** israel philharmonic renat chorus	*programme as for 20 january*

london
27 february 1964
philharmonia

mendelssohn hebrides overture/dvorak symphony 9/
rachmaninov piano concerto 2/ravel rapsodie
espagnole
simon, piano

london
1 march 1964
philharmonia
orchestra and chorus

verdi 4 pezzi sacri/brahms symphony 1
vaughan

london
5 march 1964
philharmonia

wagner tannhäuser overture/schubert symphony 8/
tchaikovsky violin concerto/rossini guglielmo tell
overture
parikian, violin

florence
15 march 1964
maggio musicale
orchestra and chorus

mozart sinfonia concertante for violin and viola/
beethoven symphony 9
*kalmus/dinato/monti/cava/abussi, violin/fotmentini,
viola*

florence
24 march 1964
maggio musicale
orchestra and chorus

mozart serenade for 13 wind/verdi 4 pezzi sacri

london
9 april 1964
philharmonia
alldis choir

vivaldi le 4 stagioni/mozart arias/stravinsky
les noces
*schwarzkopf/simon/sinclair/young/cameron/gotkovsky,
violin*

leeds
18 april 1964
philharmonia
leeds festival chorus

beethoven programme
symphony 8/symphony 9
harper/watts/neate/ward

leeds
20 april 1964
philharmonia
leeds festival chorus

haydn symphony 104/verdi 4 pezzi sacri
bosabalian
poulenc gloria in this concert was conducted by donald hunt

leeds
20 april 1964
philharmonia
leeds festival chorus

haydn symphony 104/verdi 4 pezzi sacri
bosabalian
poulenc gloria in this concert was conducted by donald hunt

leeds
21 april 1964
philharmonia

rossini semiramide overture/mozart piano concerto 22/brahms symphony 2
roll, piano

london
26 april 1964
philharmonia
orchestra and chorus

verdi messa da requiem
ligabue/bumbry/konya/arié

during the 1964 uk visit giulini also conducted three concerts for bbc television with the philharmonia orchestra: programmes comprised the last three mozart symphonies and works by falla; these took place in croydon fairfield halls and were transmitted by bbc television on 5 and 19 january and 2 february 1965; a further television concert with mozart sinfonia concertante and ravel ma mere l'oye may also have been recorded in portsmouth guildhall

rome
21 may 1964
rome opera
orchestra and chorus

mozart le nozze di figaro
ligabue (panni)/adani/malagu/panerai/trama
further performances given

scheveningen
27 june 1964
residentie orchestra
netherlands
chamber chorus

haydn symphony 104/mendelssohn violin concerto/ haydn nelson mass
de la bije/van sante/van hese/hoekman/goldberg, violin

london
19, 23, 26 and 28 november and 1, 4, 7 and 10 december 1964
covent garden
orchestra and chorus

verdi il trovatore
jones/simionato/prevedi/glossop/rouleau

rome
4 january 1965
rome opera
orchestra and chorus

mozart le nozze di figaro
ligabue (willaner)/sciutti/malagu/ganzarolli/arié
5 further performances given

chicago
28, 29 and 30
january 1965
chicago symphony

mozart programme
mauerische trauermusik/divertimento 15/symphony 41

milwaukee
1 february 1965
chicago symphony

programme as for 28, 29 and 30 january

chicago
4 and 5 february 1965
chicago symphony

respighi ancient airs and dances suite 3/schubert symphony 8/ghedini appunti per un credo/ravel rapsodie espagnole

pittsburgh
12 and 14
february 1965
pittsburgh symphony

rossini semiramide overture/prokofiev piano concerto 3/ghedini appunti per un credo/debussy la mer
bachauer, piano

pittsburgh
19 and 21
february 1965
pittsburgh symphony

verdi forza del destino overture/walton violin concerto/beethoven symphony 6
francescatti, violin

turin
26 february 1965
rai torino
orchestra and chorus

mozart programme
symphony 40/exsultate jubilate/thamos könig in ägypten
meneguzzer/zilio/frascati/monreale

milan
2 march 1965
rai milano orchestra

mozart symphony 41/haydn symphony 104

milan
5 march 1965
rai milano
orchestra and chorus

fauré requiem/debussy la mer
panni/strudthoff

naples
10 march 1965
rai napoli
orchestra and chorus

mozart divertimento 15/haydn nelson mass
arroyo/malagu/hedron/cava

rome
13 march 1965
rai roma orchestra
and chorus

schubert mass in e flat
pütz/rota/handt/benelli/cava

ein-gev
22 april 1965
israel philharmonic

ravel ma mere l'oye/brahms piano concerto 2/
mussorgsky-ravel pictures at an exhibition
barenboim, piano

tel aviv
24 april 1965
israel philharmonic

programme as for 22 april

haifa
25, 26 and 27
april 1965
israel philharmonic

programme as for 22 april

tel aviv
29 april and
1 may 1965
israel philharmonic

bach concerto for 2 violins/ravel ma mere l'oye/
mussorgsky-ravel pictures at an exhibition
tal and pianka, violins

jerusalem
2 may 1965
israel philharmonic

bach concerto for 2 violins/ravel ma mere l'oye/
brahms symphony 4
tal and pianka, violins

tel aviv
3 may 1965
israel philharmonic

mozart divertimento 11/bach concerto for 2
violins/brahms symphony 4
tal and pianka, violins

tel aviv
6 and 8 may 1965
israel philharmonic

mozart divertimento 11/bach concerto for 2
violins/mussorgsky-ravel pictures at an exhibition
tal and pianka, violins

tel aviv
9 and 11 may 1965
israel philharmonic

programme as for 3 may

rome
20 may 1965
rome opera
orchestra and chorus

verdi falstaff
berdini/ di stasio/ talarico/ fioroni (barbieri)/ alva/ gobbi/ panerai (rinaldi/ capecchi)
6 further performances given

den haag
21 june 1965
residentie orchestra
holland festival chorus

mozart don giovanni
ligabue/ bosabalian/ adani/ alva (ottolini)/ capecchi/ montarsolo/ zerbini

rotterdam
27 june 1965
residentie orchestra
holland festival chorus

programme as for 21 june

amsterdam
29 june 1965
residentie orchestra
holland festival chorus

programme as for 21 june

den haag
1 july 1965
residentie orchestra
holland festival chorus

programme as for 21 june

amsterdam
3 july 1965
residentie orchestra
holland festival chorus

programme as for 21 june

utrecht
5 july 1965
residentie orchestra
holland festival chorus

programme as for 21 june

den haag *programme as for 21 june*
9 july 1965
residentie orchestra
holland festival chorus

amsterdam *programme as for 21 june*
12 july 1965
residentie orchestra
holland festival chorus

edinburgh mozart don giovanni
23, 25 and 28 *ligabue/bosabalian/adani/lewis/capecchi/montarsolo/*
august 1965 *tadeo*
new philharmonia *these were concert performances of the opera*
netherlands
chamber chorus

edinburgh *mozart programme*
31 august 1965 divertimento 15/serenade for 13 wind
new philharmonia

edinburgh *programme as for 23 august*
1 and 3
september 1965
new philharmonia
netherlands
chamber chorus

edinburgh haydn symphony 94/beethoven piano concerto 1/
4 sepember 1965 schumann symphony 3
new philharmonia *arrau, piano*

london verdi il trovatore
25 october 1965 *jones/cossotto/bergonzi/glossop/vinco*
covent garden
orchestra and chorus

london mozart symphony 41/mozart horn concerto 4/
26 october 1965 brahms symphony 4
new philharmonia *civil, horn*

london
27 october 1965
covent garden
orchestra and chorus

programme as for 25 october

london
28 october 1965
new philharmonia

rossini semiramide overture/mozart sinfonia concertante for 4 wind/ravel ma mere l'oye/ debussy la mer
watson, oboe/walton, clarinet/brooke, bassoon/civil, horn

london
30 october 1965
covent garden
orchestra and chorus

programme as for 25 october

rome
20 and 22 november 1965
rome opera
orchestra and chorus

verdi don carlo
sarocca/parutto (simionato)/cecchele/paskalis/siepi/talvela

london
1 may 1966
new philharmonia
orchestra and chorus

brahms piano concerto 2/haydn nelson mass
lorengar/veasey/lewis/shirley-quirk/curzon, piano

london
8 may 1966
new philharmonia
orchestra and chorus

mozart programme
symphony 39/requiem
lorengar/veasey/lewis/shirley-quirk

london
12 may 1966
new philharmonia

mozart programme
serenade for 13 wind/divertimento 15

london
15 may 1966
new philharmonia
orchestra and chorus

beethoven missa solemnis
lorengar/veasey/lewis/borg

london
11 and 12 july 1966
new philharmonia
orchestra and chorus

verdi messa da requiem
jones/veasey/gedda/arié
concerts in st paul's cathedral

milan
3 and 4 october 1966
la scala orchestra
and chorus

beethoven missa solemnis
arroyo/höffgen/bottion/talvela

milan
7 and 8 october 1966
la scala orchestra

mozart programme
divertimento 15/piano concerto 27/maurerische
trauermusik/symphony 41
casadesus, piano

budapest
24 october 1966
hungarian state
symphony orchestra

dvorak symphony 7/ravel ma mere l'oye/falla el
sombrero de 3 picos

budapest
27 october 1966
hungarian state
symphony orchestra

mozart programme
divertimento 15/maurerische trauermusik/
symphony 41

rome
19 november 1966
rome opera
orchestra and chorus

verdi rigoletto
scotto (fusco)/breda/pavarotti (merighi)/paskalis (schiavi/
monachesi)/washington (pugliese)
8 further performances given

florence
16, 18, 20 and
22 december 1966
maggio musicale
orchestra and chorus

programme as for 19 november

tel aviv
14 and 15
january 1967
israel philhaemonic

mozart symphony 35/piano concerto 20/schubert
symphony 4/rossini guglielmo tell overture
michelangeli, piano

jerusalem
16 january 1967
israel philharmonic

programme as for 14 and 15 january

tel aviv
17, 18, 19 and 21
january 1967
israel philharmonic

programme as for 14 and 15 january

tel aviv
22 and 23
january 1967
israel philharmonic

mozart serenade for 13 wind/liszt piano concerto 2/
rossini guglielmo tell overture
rogoff, piano

beer sheva
24 january 1967
israel philharmonic

mozart symphony 35/schumann piano concerto/
schubert symphony 4
rogoff, piano

yagur
25 january 1967
israel philharmonic

programme as for 22 and 23 january

tel aviv
26 january 1967
israel philharmonic

programme as for 22 and 23 january

ein-gev
29 january 1967
israel philharmonic

programme as for 24 january

eilat
31 january 1967
israel philharmonic

mozart symphony 35/mozart violin concerto 3/
schubert symphony 4
markus, violin

pittsburgh
17 and 19
february 1967
pittsburgh symphony

mozart programme
divertimento 11/flute concerto 1/don giovanni
overture/symphony 39
goldberg, flute

chicago
23 and 24
february 1967
chicago symphony
orchestra and chorus

haydn symphony 95/cherubini requiem in c minor

chicago
2, 3 and 4
march 1967
chicago symphony

mozart programme
don giovanni overture/eine kleine nachtmusik/
oboe concerto/divertimento 11/symphony 39
still, oboe

chicago
9 and 10 march 1967
chicago symphony

petrassi concerto for strings/chopin piano
concerto 2/dvorak symphony 7
malcuzynski, piano

milwaukee
27 march 1967
chicago symphony
orchestra and chorus

programme as for 23 and 24 february

london
19, 24 and 26
april 1967
covent garden
orchestra and chorus

verdi la traviata
freni/cioni/cappuccilli

london
27 april 1967
new philharmonia

mozart divertimento 11/beethoven piano concerto 1/
schubert symphony 4
roll, piano

london
29 april 1967
covent garden
orchestra and chorus

programme as for 19, 24 and 26 april

london
30 april 1967
new philharmonia
orchestra and chorus

vivaldi le 4 stagioni/verdi 4 pezzi sacri
m.price/bean, violin

london *programme as for 19, 24 and 26 april*
2 may 1967
covent garden
orchestra and chorus

london haydn symphony 94/wagner wesendonk-lieder/
4 may 1967 verdi 4 pezzi sacri
new philharmonia *bjoner/m.price*
orchestra and chorus

london *programme as for 19, 24 and 26 april*
5 may 1967
covent garden
orchestra and chorus

two concerts with the new philharmonia orchestra and chorus to mark the centenary of the birth of arturo toscanini
florence beethoven missa solemnis
13 may 1967 *harper/höffgen/bottion/arié*
new philharmonia
orchestra and chorus

parma *programme as for 13 may*
14 may 1967
new philharmonia
orchestra and chorus

venice *mozart programme*
26 may 1967 maurerische trauermusik/symphony 40/requiem
la fenice orchestra *rizzoli/hamari/prior/el hage*
wiener singverein

aix bonporti concerto op 11 no 8/mozart piano
27 july 1967 concerto 26/schumann symphony 3
pasdeloup orchestra *casadesus, piano*

edinburgh **26 and 27** **august 1967** netherlands chamber orchestra new philharmonia chorus	bach mass in b minor *stadler/ baker/ lewis/ el hage*
london **24 september 1967** new philharmonia	*brahms programme* tragic overture/double concerto/symphony 1 *maguire, violin and du pré, cello*
london **28 september 1967** new philharmonia ambrosian singers	respighi ancient airs and dances suite 3/debussy 3 nocturnes/dvorak symphony 7
berlin **10 and 11** **october 1967** berlin philharmonic st hedwig's choir	verdi 4 pezzi sacri/cherubini requiem in c minor *giulini's début with the berlin philharmonic orchestra*
milan **3 and 4 november 1967** la scala orchestra and chorus	schubert symphony 4/cherubini requiem in c minor
florence **9 november 1967** maggio musicale orchestra	bonporti concerto op 11 no 8/chopin piano concerto 2/dvorak symphony 7 *tipo, piano*
florence **12 november 1967** maggio musicale orchestra and chorus	*mozart programme* maurerische trauermusik/symphony 40/requiem *stich-randall/ rota/ grimaldi/ arié*
modena **13 november 1967** la scala orchestra and chorus	*programme as for 3 and 4 november*

treviso
14 november 1967
la scala orchestra
and chorus

cherubini requiem in c minor
arturo toscanini commemoration concert

croydon
18 november 1967
new philharmonia
orchestra and chorus

brahms alto rhapsody/dvorak symphony 7/brahms
symphony 4
baker

london
26 november 1967
new philharmonia

tchaikovsky symphony 2/prokofiev piano concerto 3/
mussorgsky-ravel pictures at an exhibition
krainov, piano

london
30 november 1967
new philharmonia
orchestra and chorus

brahms programme
alto rhapsody/violin concerto/symphony 4
baker/ughi, violin

pittsburgh
10 and 12
december 1967
pittsburgh symphony

rossini guglielmo tell overture/tchaikovsky violin
concerto/dvorak symphony 7
szeryng, violin

rome
16 december 1967
rai roma orchestra

mozart serenade for 13 wind/brahms symphony 1

rome
22 december 1967
rai roma orchestra
and chorus

schubert symphony 4/rossini stabat mater
zylis-gara/verrett/pavarotti/zaccaria

london
16 january 1968
new philharmonia
orchestra and chorus

schubert symphony 5/britten building of the house
overture/rossini stabat mater
bosabalian/troyanos/bottion/el hage

london **21 january 1968** new philharmonia orchestra and chorus	beethoven symphony 6/cherubini requiem in c minor
turin **26 january 1968** rai torino orchestra and chorus	beethoven egmont overture/beethoven piano concerto 4/cherubini requiem in c minor *weissenberg, piano*
tel aviv **13 february 1968** israel philharmonic	mozart maurerische trauermusik/beethoven violin concerto/debussy la mer/britten young person's guide *menuhin, violin*
jerusalem **14 february 1968** israel philharmonic	*programme as for 13 february*
tel aviv **15, 18 and 19** **february 1968** israel philharmonic	*programme as for 13 february*
haifa **20, 21 and 22** **february 1968** israel philharmonic	mozart maurerische trauermusik/brahms violin concerto/debussy la mer/britten young person's guide *menuhin, violin*
tel aviv **24 february 1968** israel philharmonic	brahms tragic overture/mendelssohn violin concerto/ brahms violin concerto *menuhin, violin*
jerusalem **25 february 1968** israel philharmonic	*programme as for 20, 21 and 22 february*
tel aviv **26 february 1968** israel philharmonic	*programme as for 13 february*

tel aviv *ptogramme as for 20, 21 and 22 february*
27, 28 and 29
february 1968
israel philharmonic

croydon *verdi programme*
3 march 1968 vespri siciliani overture/4 pezzi sacri
new philharmonia *bbc television*
orchestra and chorus

rome cherubini requiem in c minor/brahms symphony 2
13 march 1968
santa cecilia
orchestra and chorus

london *brahms programme*
21 april 1968 symphony 3/piano concerto 1
new philharmonia *curzon, piano*

london *brahms programme*
25 april 1968 piano concerto 2/symphony 2
new philharmonia *curzon, piano*

florence mozart symphony 39/rossini stabat mater
18 may 1968 *ross/verrett/ottolini/raimondi*
maggio musicale
orchestra and chorus

budapest *brahms programme*
24 may 1968 piano concerto 1/symphony 1
new philharmonia *curzon, piano*

budapest haydn symphony 94/britten les illuminations/
25 may 1968 beethoven symphony 6
new philharmonia *vyvyan*

bratislava haydn symphony 94/britten les illuminations/
27 may 1968 dvorak symphony 7
new philharmonia *vyvyan*

prague　　　　　　　　　haydn symphony 104/britten les illuminations/
29 may 1968　　　　　　dvorak symphony 7
new philharmonia　　　　　*vyvyan*

prague　　　　　　　　　*programme as for 24 may*
30 may 1968
new philharmonia

new york　　　　　　　　mozart le nozze di figaro
22, 24, 26 and　　　　　*ligabue/sciutti/casoni/panerai/gobbi*
29 june 1968　　　　　　*guest performances by rome opera at the metropolitan*
rome opera　　　　　　　　*opera house*
orchestra and chorus　　　　*giulini's final appearances with the rome opera*

london　　　　　　　　　beethoven missa solemnis
16 july 1968　　　　　　*zylis-gara/höffgen/tear/arié*
new philharmonia　　　　　*concert in st paul's cathedral*
and chorus

london　　　　　　　　　verdi messa da requiem
19 july 1968　　　　　　*bosabalian/hamari/bottion/arié*
new philharmonia　　　　　*concert in st paul's cathedral*
and chorus

edinburgh　　　　　　　*schubert programme*
31 august 1968　　　　　symphony 4/mass in e flat
new philharmonia　　　　　*pashley/michelow/hughes/robertson/mccue*
scottish festival chorus

edinburgh　　　　　　　britten war requiem
1 september 1968　　　　*vishnevskaya/pears/fischer-dieskau*
new philharmonia　　　　　*melos ensemble conducted by the composer*
scottish festival chorus

rome　　　　　　　　　　bonporti concerto op 11 no 8/haydn symphony 94/
20 september 1968　　　　brahms symphony 2
rai roma orchestra

ferrara　　　　　　　　　respighi ancient airs and dances suite 3/schubert
17 october 1968　　　　　symphony 8/weber freischütz overture/brahms
rai roma orchestra　　　　　symphony 2

new york | *mozart programme*
12, 13, 14 and | diverimento 11/piano concerto 20/symphony 40/
16 december 1968 | maurerische trauermusik
new york philharmonic | *michelangeli, piano*

new york | hindemith concert music for strings and brass/
19, 20, 21 and | martinu piano concerto 2/brahms symphony 1
30 december 1968 | *firkusny, piano*
new york philharmonic

new york | bonporti concerto op 11 no 8/schubert symphony 4/
2, 3, 4 and 6 | verdi 4 pezzi sacri
january 1969
new york philharmonic
camerata singers

new york | haydn symphony 94/casella la giara/schumann
9, 10, 11 and | symphony 3
13 january 1969
new york philharmonic

croydon | schubert symphony 5/beethoven symphony 9
1 february 1969 | *m.price/veasey/shirley/ridderbusch*
new philharmonia
orchestra and chorus

london | hindemith concert music for strings and brass/
4 february 1969 | schumann piano concerto/dvorak symphony 7
new philharmonia | *barenboim, piano*

berlin | rossini semiramide overture/schubert symphony 4/
13 and 15 | franck psyché et éros/debussy la mer
february 1969
berlin philharmonic

chicago
6, 7 and 8
march 1969
chicago symphony
orchestra and chorus

schubert symphony 5/prokofiev sinfonia concertante
for cello and orchestra/franck psyché et éros/
debuusy 3 nocturnes/weber freischütz overture
rostropovich, cello

chicago
10 march 1969
chicago symphony
orchestra and chorus

schubert symphony 5/sibelius violin concerto/
franck psyché et éros/debussy 3 nocturnes/weber
freischütz overture
weiss, violin

chicago
13 and 14 march 1969
chicago symphony
orchestra and chorus

mozart programme
serenade for 13 wind/requiem
tyler/simon/kolk/paul

philadelphia
20, 21, 22 and
24 march 1969
philadelphia orchestra

schubert symphony 5/rossini semiramide overture/
brahms symphony 2

new york
25 march 1969
philadelphia orchestra

programme as for 20, 21, 22 and 24 march

london
6 april 1969
new philharmonia
orchestra and chorus
melos ensemble

britten war requiem
woytowicz/pears/wilbrink
melos ensemble conducted by the composer

london
10 april 1969
new philharmonia

casella la giara/mozart piano concerto 21/franck
symphony in d minor
orozco, piano

tel aviv
17, 19, 20, 24 and
26 april 1969
israel philharmonic
tel aviv chorus

beethoven missa solemnis
harper/reynolds/mitchinson/arié

jerusalem
27 april 1969
israel philharmonic
tel aviv chorus

programme as for 17, 19, 20, 24 and 26 april

tel aviv
29 april and
1 and 3 may 1969
israel philharmonic
tel aviv chorus

programme as for 17, 19, 20, 24 and 26 april

yagur
5 may 1969
israel philharmonic
tel aviv chorus

programme as for 17, 19, 20, 24 and 26 april

beer sheva
7 may 1969
israel philharmonic

gluck iphigénie en tauride overture/arias by bach,
gluck and verdi/brahms symphony 1
guy

tel aviv
8 may 1969
israel philharmonic

programme as for 7 may

london
25 may 1969
new philharmonia

schubert symphony 5/britten les illuminations/
berlioz orchestral extracts from roméo et juliette
vyvyan

london
27 may 1969
new philharmonia

bonporti concerto op 11 no 8/britten serenade for
tenor, horn and strings/berlioz orchestral extracts
from roméo et juliette
pears/tuckwell, horn

ely
25 june 1969
new philharmonia

schubert symphony 5/britten serenade for tenor,
horn and strings/berlioz orchestral extracts from
roméo et juliette
pears/tuckwell, horn

bristol
27 june 1969
new philharmonia

bonporti concerto op 11 no 8/beethoven piano
concerto 4/britten les illuminations/schubert
symphony 4
vyvyan/curzon, piano

bath
28 june 1969
new philharmonia
orchestra and chorus

beethoven missa solemnis
m.price/baker/tear/grant

edinburgh
9 september 1969
new philharmonia
scottish festival chorus

bonporti concerto op 11 no 8/petrassi magnificat/
rossini stabat mater
gayer/gulin/baker/gedda/arié

edinburgh
12 and 13
september 1969
new philharmonia
orchestra and chorus

verdi messa da requiem
gulin/verrett/gedda/arié

chicago
25, 26 and 27
september 1969
chicago symphony

berlioz orchestral extracts from roméo et juliette/
salviucci introduzione passacaglia e finale/
stravinsky petrushka

iowa city
29 september 1969
chicago symphony

programme as for 25, 26 and 27 september

chicago
2 and 3 october 1969
chicago symphony

beethoven egmont overture/beethoven violin
concerto/hindemith concert music for strings and
brass/stravinsky petrushka
stern, violin

milwaukee
6 october 1969
chicago symphony

programme as for 2 and 3 october

chicago
9, 10 and 11
october 1969
chicago symphony

bonporti concerto op 11 no 8/beethoven piano
concerto 1/brahms symphony 4
frank, piano

chicago
16, 17 and 18
october 1969
chicago symphony

rossini semiramide overture/paganini violin concerto 2/
mussorgsky khovantschina prelude/mussorgsky-ravel
pictures at an exhibition
gulli, violin

boston
31 october and
1 and 4
november 1969
boston symphony

bonporti concerto op 11 no 8/schubert symphony 4/
pizzetti fedra prelude/mussorgsky-ravel pictures ar
exhibition

providence
6 november 1969
boston symphony

programme as for 31 october and 1 and 4 november

boston
7, 8 and 11
november 1969
boston symphony

haydn symphony 94/casella la giara/brahms symphony 4

croydon
22 november 1969
new philharmonia

salviucci introduzione passacaglia e finale/sibelius
violin concerto/schumann symphony 3
i.oistrakh, violin

london
23 november 1969
new philharmonia

programme as for 22 november

london
27 november 1969
new philharmonia

hindemith concert music for strings and brass/
prokofiev piano concerto 3/dvorak symphony 7
ashkenazy, piano

london
30 november 1969
new philharmonia

hindemith concert music for strings and brass/
beethoven piano concerto 3/dvorak symphony 7
ashkenazy, piano

berlin
5 and 7
december 1969
berlin philharmonic

beethoven egmont overture/beethoven symphony 6/
mussorgsky-ravel pictures at an exhibtion

rome
20 december 1969
rai roma orchestra
and chorus

beethoven missa solemnis
arroyo/hamari/hollweg/roida

chicago
29, 30 and 31
january 1970
chicago symphony

casella la giara/chopin piano concerto 2/brahms
symphony 3
arrau, piano

milwaukee
2 february 1970
chicago symphony

programme as for 29, 30 and 31 january

chicago
5 and 6
february 1970
chicago symphony

mozart le nozze di figaro overture/brahms violin
concerto/nabokov 2 portraits/debussy la mer
francescatti, violin

chicago
12, 13 and 14
february 1970
chicago symphony
orchestra and chorus

beethoven missa solemnis
zylis-gara/reynolds/tear/flagello

chicago
19, 20 and 21
february 1970
chicago symphony

mozart symphony 35/mozart piano concerto 18/
schumann symphony 3
anda, piano

milwaukee
23 february 1970
chicago symphony

programme as for 19, 20 and 21 february

rome | mozart don giovanni
7 april 1970 | *jurinac/janowitz/miljakovic/kraus/ghiaurov/bruscantini/petkov*
rai roma orchestra and chorus | *this was probably a concert performance of the opera*

madrid | dvorak symphony 7/mussorgsky khovantschina
17, 18 and 19 april 1970 | prelude/mussorgsky-ravel pictures at an exhibition
spanish national orchestra |

london | brahms piano concerto 1/franck psyché et éros/
28 april 1970 | debussy la mer
new philharmonia | *orozco, piano*

london | rossini semiramide overture/paganini violin
30 april 1970 | concerto 2/mussorgsky khovantschina prelude/
new philharmonia | mussorgsky-ravel pictures at an exhibition
| *gulli, violin*

suresnes | beethoven egmont overture/beethoven violin
26 may 1970 | concerto/salviucci introduzione passacaglia e
orchestre de paris | finale/stravinsky firebird suite
| *szeryng, violin*

paris | *programme as for 26 may*
27 may 1970
orchestre de paris

rosny-sous-bois | *programme as for 26 may*
28 may 1970
orchestre de paris

metz | *programme as for 26 may*
29 may 1970
orchestre de paris

london   *concert in st paul's cathedral*
6 july 1970
new philharmonia
orchestra and chorus

london   martin maria triptychon/mozart requiem
8 july 1970   *seefried; schneiderhan, violin*
new philharmonia   *soloists for requiem inclded baker/tear/rintzler*
orchestra and chorus   *concert in st paul's cathedral*

salzburg   rossini semiramide overture/schubert symphony 4/
5 august 1970   franck psyché et éros/debussy la mer
berlin philharmonic

edinburgh   beethoven missa solemnis
27 august 1970   *harper/baker/domingo/el hage*
new philharmonia
edinburgh festival chorus

edinburgh   haydn symphony 99/mahler kindertotenlieder/
4 september 1970   schumann symphony 3
london philharmonic   *fischer-dieskau*

edinburgh   *beethoven programme*
6 september 1970   egmont overture/piano concerto 4/symphony 7
london philharmonic   *curzon, piano*

london   vivaldi le 4 stagioni/beethoven mass in c
20 september 1970   *ameling/baker/altmeyer/rintzler/hurwitz, violin*
new philharmonia
orchestra and chorus

chicago   frescobaldi-ghedini 3 pieces for orchestra/martin
24 and 25   petite symphonie concertante/beethoven symphony 7
september 1970
chicago symphony

chicago   vivaldi le 4 stagioni/mozart piano concerto 9/
1, 2 and 3   ravel rapsodie espagnole
october 1970   *browning, piano and weiss, violin*
chicago symphony

milwaukee
5 october 1970
chicago symphony

programme as for 1, 2 and 3 october

chicago
8 and 9 october 1970
chicago symphony

cimarosa oboe concerto/prokofiev piano concerto 2/
dvorak symphony 7
orozco, piano and still, oboe

chicago
15, 16 and 17 october 1970
chicago symphony orchestra and chorus

haydn symphony 99/beethoven mass in c
zylis-gara/simon/alva/plishka

milwaukee
19 october 1970
chicago symphony

programme as for 8 and 9 october

florence
31 october and 3 november 1970
maggio musicale orchestra and chorus

mozart symphony 41/beethoven symphony 9
donath/reynolds/baratti/arié

florence
7 and 8 november 1970
maggio musicale orchestra and chorus

verdi messa da requiem
molnar-talajic/cossotto/bottion/arié

london
6 december 1970
new philharmonia orchestra and chorus

frescobaldi-ghedini 3 pieces for orchestra/petrassi
magnificat/verdi 4 pezzi sacri
hill

london
13 december 1970
new philharmonia

weber freischütz overture/berlioz les nuits d'été/
mahler symphony 1
baker

london
16 december 1970
new philharmonia
orchestra and chorus

beethoven missa solemnis
arroyo/reynolds/tear/rintzler
beethoven bi-centenary concert for the royal philharmonic society

cologne
15 january 1971
wdr orchestra

beethoven egmont overture/mendelssohn violin concerto/franck psyché et éros/debussy la mer
zukerman, violin

los angeles
18 and 19
february 1971
los angeles philharmonic

berlioz orchestral excerpts from roméo et juliette/brahms piano concerto 1
brendel, piano

santa monica
21 february 1971
los angeles philharmonic

programme as for 18 and 19 february

pasadena
24 february 1971
los angeles philharmonic

busoni sarabande und cortege/mahler symphony 1/mendelssohn violin concerto
zukerman, violin

los angeles
25, 26 and 29
february 1971
los angeles philharmonic

programme as for 24 february

chicago
4, 5 and 6 march 1971
chicago symphony

mozart programme
ein musikalischer spass/sinfonia concertante for 4 winds/symphony 39

chicago
11 and 12 march 1971
chicago symphony
orchestra and chorus

rayki concert requiem/beethoven piano concerto 2/denniston sun song/brahms tragic overture
j.lewenthal, piano

chicago
13 march 1971
chicago symphony

mozart le nozze di figaro overture/arias by mozart and barber/strauss 4 letzte lieder/berlioz orchestral excerpts from roméo et juliette
l.price

milwaukee
15 march 1971
chicago symphony

programme as for 13 march

chicago
18 and 19 march 1971
chicago symphony

mozart adagio and fugue in c minor/mozart violin
concerto 4/mahler symphony 1
zukerman, violin

chicago
25, 26 and 27 march 1971
chicago symphony
orchestra and chorus

verdi messa da requiem
arroyo/verrett/cossutta/flagello

berlin
16 and 18 april 1971
berlin philharmonic
ernst-senff-chor

vivaldi le 4 stagioni/beethoven mass in c
donath/fassbänder/grobe/ridderbusch

berlin
22 april 1971
berlin philharmonic

haydn symphony 94/salviucci introduzione
passacaglia e finale/schumann symphony 3

vienna
12 and 13 may 1971
vienna symphony

brahms piano concerto 1/franck psyché et éros/
mussorgsky-ravel pictures at an exhibition
dichter, piano

zürich
15 june 1971
tonhalle-orchester

rossini semiramide overture/mozart piano
concerto 24/dvorak symphony 7
curzon, piano

york
10 july 1971
new philharmonia
orchestra and chorus

beethoven missa solemnis
june/baker/tear/estes

orange
25 july 1971
orchestre de paris
new philharmonia chorus

verdi messa da requiem
gulin/ ludwig/ gedda/ talvela

salzburg
25 august 1971
vienna philharmonic

haydn symphony 94/salviucci introduzione
passacaglia e finale/brahms symphony 4
giulini's first appearance with vienna philharmonic orchestra

european tour with chicago symphony orchestra; other concerts on this tour conducted by georg solti

edinburgh
6 september 1971
chicago symphony

berlioz orchestral extracts from roméo et juliette/
mozart symphony 39/stravinsky firebird suite

edinburgh
7 september 1971
chicago symphony

brahms tragic overture/ptokofiev piano concerto 2/
haydn symphony 94/ravel rapsodie espagnole
orozco, piano

gent
9 september 1971
chicago symphony

mozart symphony 39/mahler symphony 1

helsinki
13 september 1971
chicago symphony

haydn symphony 94/mahler symphony 1

stockholm
15 september 1971
chicago symphony

mozart symphony 39/beethoven symphony 7

berlin
21 september 1971
chicago symphony

programme as for 15 september

vienna
26 september 1971
chicago symphony

haydn symphony 94/stravinsky firebird suite/
berlioz orchestral extracts from roméo et juliette

paris haydn symphony 94/brahms tragic overture/
3 october 1971 beethoven symphony 7
chicago symphony

london *programme as for 15 september*
5 october 1971
chicago symphony

florence mahler symphony 9
13 and 14
november 1971
maggio musicale
orchestra

chicago albert leaves from the golden notebook/mozart
2 and 3 piano concerto 24/brahms symphony 2
december 1971 *watts, piano*
chicago symphony

milwaukee rossini semiramide overture/albert leaves from the
6 december 1971 golden notebook/brahms symphony 2
chicago symphony

chicago mahler symphony 9
9, 10 and 11
december 1971
chicago symphony

chicago bach mass in b minor
16, 17 and 18 *m.price/veasey/alva/shirley-quirk*
december 1971
chicago symphony
orchestra and chorus

chicago bach violin concerto 2/mozart sinfonia concertante
13 and 14 for violin and viola/beethoven symphony 6
january 1972 *goldberg, violin and preves, viola*
chicago symphony

chicago
20, 21 and 22
january 1972
chicago symphony

shostakovich symphony 14/tchaikovsky symphony 2
curtin/arié

chicago
27, 28 and 29
january 1972
chicago symphony

ghedini concerto da camera/turchi il labirinto/
beethoven violin concerto
goldberg, violin

milwaukee
31 january 1972
chicago symphony

programme as for 27, 28 and 29 january

chicago
3, 4 and 5
february 1972
chicago symphony
orchestra and chorus

mozart symphony 40/wilfred josephs requiem
arié

illinois
7 and 9 february 1972
chicago symphony

ghedini concerto da camera/turchi il labirinto/
tchaikovsky symphony 2

philadelphia
3, 4 and 6
march 1972
philadelphia orchestra

beethoven egmont overture/beethoven piano
concerto 4/turchi il labirinto/falla el sombrero de
3 picos
weissenberg, piano

philadelphia
9, 10 and 11
march 1972
philadelphia orchestra

haydn symphony 94/albert leaves from the golden
notebook/berlioz orchestral extracts from roméo
et juliette

philadelphia
16, 17 and 18
march 1972
philadelphia orchestra

mahler symphony 9

new york
21 march 1972
philadelphia orchestra

programme as for 16, 17 and 18 march

berlin
9 and 10 april 1972
berlin philharmonic

brahms programme
symphony 3/piano concerto 2
arrau, piano

berlin
13 and 14 april 1972
berlin philharmonic

mahler symphony 9

venice
14 may 1972
la fenice orchestra

schubert symphony 4/brahms symphony 2

paris
23, 24 and 25
may 1972
orchestre de paris

beethoven piano concerto 4/mahler symphony 1
weissenberg, piano

yerres
26 may 1972
orchestre de paris

programme as for 23, 24 and 25 may

amsterdam
5 july 1972
concertgebouw
orchestra

haydn symphony 94/turchi il labirinto/berlioz
orchestral extracts from roméo et juliette

rotterdam
6 july 1972
concertgebouw
orchestra

programme as for 5 july

orange
16 july 1972
orchestre de paris
new philharmonia chorus

bach mass in b minor
mathis/ludwig/alva/shirley-quirk

munich
10 august 1972
vienna symphony

rossini semiramide overture/schubert symphony 4/
brahms symphony 2

bregenz
15 august 1972
vienna symphony

programme as for 10 august

edinburgh
27 august 1972
london philharmonic

shostakovich symphony 14/tchaikovsky symphony 2
woytowicz/arié

edinburgh
31 august 1972
london philharmonic

mahler symphony 9

chicago
28, 29 and 30
september 1972
chicago symphony

schumann manfred overture/petrassi concerto for
strings/brahms symphony 1

chicago
5 and 6 october 1972
chicago symphony

beethoven piano concerto 3/shostakovich symphony 8
lupu, piano

chicago
12, 13 and 14
october 1972
chicago symphony
orchestra and chorus

vivaldi bassoon concerto in b flat/vivaldi gloria/
rossini stabat mater
harper/hamari/luchetti/arié/elliott, bassoon

milwaukee
16 october 1972
chicago symphony

programme as for 5 and 6 october

chicago
19 and 20
october 1972
chicago symphony

lombardo threnody for strings/lalo cello concerto/
ravel ma mere l'oye/falla el sombrero de 3 picos
miller, cello

chicago
21 october 1972
chicago symphony

brahms piano concerto 2/beethoven symphony 7
barenboim, piano

london
21 november 1972
london symphony

schumann manfred overture/petrassi concerto for strings/brahms symphony 2

london
26 november 1972
london symphony
orchestra and chorus

beethoven programme
symphony 8/symphony 9
armstrong/reynolds/tear/shirley-quirk

london
9 january 1973
london symphony
orchestra and chorus

beethoven missa solemnis
harwood/watts/tear/howell
concert in st paul's cathedral

den bosch
25 january 1973
concertgebouw
orchestra

schumann manfred overture/petrassi concerto for strings/dvorak symphony 7

den haag
26 january 1973
concertgebouw
orchestra

programme as for 25 january

amsterdam
28 and 29
january 1973
concertgebouw
orchestra

programme as for 25 january

amsterdam
31 january and
1 february 1973
concertgebouw
orchestra

shostakovich symphony 14/tchaikovsky symphony 2
woytowicz/arié

stockholm
7, 8 and 9
february 1973
swedish radio orchestra

mahler symphony 9

philadelphia
8, 9 and 10
march 1973
philadelphia orchestra

brahms piano concerto 2/mahler symphony 1
orozco, piano

new york
12 march 1973
philadelphia orchestra

programme as for 8, 9 and 10 march

philadelphia
15, 16, 17 and
20 march 1973
philadelphia orchestra

haydn sinfonia concertante/debussy la mer/
tchaikovsky symphony 2

berlin
4 and 6 may 1973
berlin philharmonic
ernst-senff-chor

schumann manfred overture/petrassi concerto for
strings/schubert mass in e flat
lorengar/wagner/hollweg/ellenbeck/van dam

berlin
9 and 11 may 1973
berlin philharmonic

mussorgsky khovantschina prelude/tchaikovsky
violin concerto/dvorak symphony 7
chung, violin

paris
22, 23 and 24
may 1973
orchestre de paris

prokofiev piano concerto 2/brahms symphony 1
orozco, piano

caen
25 may 1973
orchestre de paris

programme as for 22, 23 and 24 may

vienna
2 june 1973
vienna symphony

mozart eine kleine nachtmusik/mozart piano
concerto 25/ravel ma mere l'oye/debussy la mer
brendel, piano

chicago
13 june 1973
chicago symphony

rossini semiramide overture/debussy la mer/brahms symphony no 4

vienna virginia
15 june 1973
chicago symphony

programme as for 13 june

vienna virginia
16 june 1973
chicago symphony

mussorgsky khovantschina prelude/mussorgsky-ravel pictures at an exhibition/schumann symphony 3

orange
15 july 1973
orchestre de paris
new philharmonia chorus

beethoven missa solemnis
moser/hesse/laubenthal/howell

edinburgh
23 august 1973
london symphony
edinburgh festival chorus

schumann das paradies und die peri
mathis/armstrong/pears/rolfe-johnson/brendel/allen

edinburgh
24 august 1973
london symphony

webern passacaglia/mozart piano concerto 20/schubert symphony 9
a.fischer, piano

montreux
30 september 1973
vienna symphony

mozart symphony 40/mozart violin concerto 1/schumann symphony 3
sivo, violin

turin
1 october 1973
vienna symphony

programme as for 30 september

paris
10, 11 and 13 october 1973
orchestre de paris
new philharmonia chorus

verdi messa da requiem
scotto/cossotto/bergonzi/arié

lille
19 october 1973
orchestre de paris

mozart le nozze di figaro overture/mozart piano concerto 20/beethoven symphony 7
frantz, piano

paris
22 october 1973
orchestre de paris

webern programme
passacaglia/5 pieces op 10/6 pieces op 6

paris
23, 24, 25 and
27 october 1973
orchestre de paris

mozart le nozze di figaro overture/mozart piano concerto 20/webern passacaglia/debussy la mer
ashkenazy, piano

chicago
21, 23 and 24
november 1973
chicago symphony

haydn sinfonia concertante/schubert symphony 9

milwaukee
26 november 1973
chicago symphony

programme as for 21, 23 and 24 october

chicago
29 and 30
november and
1 december 1973
chicago symphony

debussy clarinet rhapsody/ravel left hand piano concerto/webern passacaglia/hindemith mathis der maler symphony
block, piano and brody, clarinet

philadelphia
6, 7 and 8
december 1973
philadelphia orchestra

vivaldi le 4 stagioni/schubert symphony 8

new york
10 december 1973
philadelphia orchestra

programme as for 6, 7 and 8 december

rome
2 february 1974
rai roma orchestra

beethoven symphony 8/schubert symphony 9

rome
9 february 1974
rai roma orchestra
and chorus

schumann das paradies und die peri
m.price/miljakovic/hollweg/brendel/el hage

chicago
14, 15 and 16
march 1974
chicago symphony

beethoven piano concerto 3/bruckner symphony 2
ciani, piano

milwaukee
18 march 1974
chicago symphony

programme as for 14, 15 and 16 march

chicago
21, 22 and 23
march 1974
chicago symphony
orchestra and chorus

schumann das paradies und die peri
norman/finnilä/haefliger/arié/creech

boston
28, 29 and 30
march and
2 april 1974
boston symphony

webern passacaglia/hindemith mathis der maler
symphony/bruckner symphony 2

boston
4 and 5 april 1974
boston symphony
tanglewood chorus

vivaldi le 4 stagioni/rossini stabat mater
phillips/clickner/wilder/hale

pasadena
7, 8 and 9
april 1974
vienna symphony

beethoven egmont overture/stravinsky firebird
suite/brahms symphony 1

vienna
14 april 1974
vienna symphony

weber freischütz overture/dvorak cello concerto/
j.strauss kaiserwalzer/stravinsky firebird suite
schafran, cello

vienna
19, 20 and 21
may 1974
vienna symphony

beethoven symphony 8/mahler symphony 1

vienna
25 and 26 may 1974
vienna symphony

beethoven violin concerto/brahms symphony 1
d.oistrakh, violin

milan
28, 29 and 30
may 1974
vienna symphony

programme as for 19, 20 and 21 may

vienna
5 and 6 june 1974
vienna symphony

schumann piano concerto/bruckner symphony 2
pollini, piano

zürich
9 june 1974
tonhalle-orchester

schumann piano concerto/bruckner symphony 2
cherkassky, piano

edinburgh
20 and 21
august 1974
london philharmonic
edinburgh festival chorus

verdi messa da requiem
arroyo (hunter)/ cossotto/ pavarotti/ arié

european tour by vienna symphony orchestra
dubrovnik
25 august 1974
vienna symphony

rossini semiramide overture/mozart piano
concerto 20/brahms symphony 1
brendel, piano

stockholm
27 august 1974
vienna symphony

rossini semiramide overture/mozart piano
concerto 20/bruckner symphony 2
brendel, piano

helsinki
28 august 1974
vienna symphony

j.c.bach sinfonia concertante/hindemith mathis
der maler symphony/bruckner symphony 2

helsinki
29 august 1974
vienna symphony

beethoven egmont overture/hindemith mathis der maler symphony/brahms symphony 1

den haag
30 august 1974
vienna symphony

programme as for 29 august

edinburgh
1 september 1974
vienna symphony

j.c.bach sinfonia concertante/hindemith mathis der maler symphony/mahler symphony 1

edinburgh
2 september 1974
vienna symphony

beethoven piano concerto 4/bruckner symphony 2
weissenberg, piano

linz
3 september 1974
vienna symphony

programme as for 27 august

new york
17, 18, 19 and
22 october 1974
new york philharmonic

mozart symphony 39/bruckner symphony 9

new york
24, 25 and 26
october 1974
new york philharmonic

brahms programme
symphony 4/piano concerto 1
firkusny, piano

chicago
31 october and
1 and 2 november 1974
chicago symphony

bach brandenburg concerto 3/bruckner symphony 9

milwaukee **4 november 1974** chicago symphony	*programme as for 31 october and 1 and 2 november*
chicago **7, 8 and 9** **november 1974** chicago symphony	stravinsky octet/prokofiev piano concerto 5/ shostakovich symphony 1 *ashkenazy, piano*
vienna **4, 5 and 6** **december 1974** vienna symphony wiener singverein	gabrieli sonata pian e forte/gabrieli canzon a 2/ mozart piano concerto 27/schubert mass in e flat *ameling/lilowa/krenn/partridge/schenk/curzon, piano*
paris **17, 18, 19 and** **21 december 1974** orchestre de paris new philharmonia chorus	beethoven missa solemnis *moser/veasey/schreier/crass*

tour of austria, germany, belgium and netherlands by vienna symphony orchestra

vienna **10, 11 and 12** **january 1975** vienna symphony	webern 6 pieces op 6/mozart sinfonia concertante for wind/dvorak symphony 7
graz **13 and 14** **january 1975** vienna symphony	webern 6 pieces op 6/ravel daphnis et chloé second suite/dvorak symphony 7
innsbruck **15 january 1975** vienna symphony	beethoven symphony 6/von einem sinfonische szenen/ravel daphnis et chloé second suite
salzburg **16 january 1975** vienna symphony	*programme as for 15 january*

linz
17 january 1975
vienna symphony

beethoven symphony 6/dvorak symphony 7

nürnberg
20 january 1975
vienna symphony

programme as for 15 january

augsburg
21 january 1975
vienna symphony

programme as for 15 january

frankfurt
22 january 1975
vienna symphony

beethoven egmont overture/mozart sinfonia concertante for wind/brahms symphony 1

hannover
23 january 1975
vienna symphony

webern 6 pieces op 6/ravel daphnis et chloé second suite/beethoven symphony 6

hamburg
24 january 1975
vienna symphony

programme as for 17 january

leverkusen
27 january 1975
vienna symphony

j.c.bach sinfonia concertante/von einem sinfonische szenen/webern 6 pieces op 6/beethoven symphony 6

stuttgart
28 january 1975
vienna symphony

programme as for 22 january

heilbronn
29 january 1975
vienna symphony

beethoven symphony 6/brahms symphony 1

wuppertal
30 january 1975
vienna symphony

programme as for 17 january

brussels
31 january 1975
vienna symphony

webern 6 pieces op 6/mozart sinfonia concertante for wind/brahms symphony 1

amsterdam
1 february 1975
vienna symphony

programme as for 17 january

rotterdam
2 february 1975
vienna symphony

programme as for 31 january

vienna
7, 8 and 9
february 1975
vienna symphony

beethoven symphony 6/prokofiev violin concerto 2/ ravel daphnis et chloé second suite
kremer, violin

munich
20 and 21 february 1975
bavarian radio orchestra

beethoven symphony 6/webern passacaglia/ stravinsky firebird suite

los angeles
13, 14 and 16
march 1975
los angeles philharmonic

mahler symphony 9

santa barbara
19 march 1975
los angeles philharmonic

brahms symphony 4/mozart symphony 39/ravel rapsodie espagnole

los angeles
20, 21 and 23
march 1975
los angeles philharmonic

programme as for 19 march

chicago
27, 28 and 29
march 1975
chicago symphony

mahler symphony 9

milwaukee
31 march 1975
chicago symphony

programme as for 27, 28 and 29 march

chicago
3, 4 and 5
april 1975
chicago symphony
orchestra and chorus

vivaldi concerti for 2, 3 and 4 violins/schubert
mass in e flat
curtin/stapp/johnson/mccollum/plishka

london
4 may 1975
london philharmonic
new philharmonia chorus

beethoven missa solemnis
harper/baker/tear/sotin

london
8 and 11 may 1975
london philharmonic

mahler symphony 9

london
14 may 1975
london philharmonic

beethoven egmont overture/berlioz les nuits d'été/
schubert symphony 9
baker

vienna
26 may 1975
vienna symphony

j.strauss donauwalzer/mahler symphony 9

prague
27 may 1975
vienna symphony

programme as for 26 may

prague
28 may 1975
vienna symphony

von einem sinfonische szenen/stravinsky firebird suite/dvorak symphony 7

zürich
3 june 1975
tonhalle-orchester

schumann manfred overture/memdelssohn violin concerto/brahms symphony 2
stern, violin

vienna
22 june 1975
vienna symphony
vienna opera chorus

beethoven missa solemnis
donath/hamari/hollweg/thomaschke

edinburgh
26 august 1975
london philharmonic
edinburgh festival chorus

mozart sinfonia concertante for wind/beethoven symphony 9
donath/hodgson/rolfe-johnson/rintzler

edinburgh
27 august 1975
london philharmonic
edinburgh festival chorus

haydn sinfonia concertante/beethoven symphony 9
donath/hodgson/rolfe-johnson/rintzler

tour of japan by vienna symphony orchestra
osaka
29 september 1975
vienna symphony

webern passacaglia/mozart symphony 40/brahms symphony 1

osaka
30 september 1975
vienna symphony

beethoven piano concerto 5/mahler symphony 1
buchbinder, piano

nagoya
2 october 1975
vienna symphony

beethoven egmont overture/mozart symphony 41/stravinsky firebird suite

tokyo
3 october 1975
vienna symphony

programme as for 29 september

tokyo
5 october 1975
vienna symphony

programme as for 30 september

tokyo
6 october 1975
vienna symphony

beethoven egmont overture/beethoven piano concerto 5/mozart symphony 41
buchbinder, piano

new york
24 october 1975
vienna symphony
temple university choir

von einem an die nachgeborenen/beethoven symphony 7
hamari/fischer-dieskau
concert for united nations assembly

vienna
26 october 1975
vienna symphony
wiener singverein

von einem an die nachgeborenen/beethoven symphony 7
hamari/krause

vienna
31 october and
2 and 3
november 1975
vienna symphony
wiener singverein

mozart symphony 41/von einem an die nachgeborenen
hamari/krause

rome
29 and 30
november 1975
santa cecilia orchestra

bruckner symphony 8

chicago
4, 5 and 6
december 1975
chicago symphony

bruckner symphony 8

milwaukee
8 december 1975
chicago symphony

programme as for 4, 5 and 6 december

chicago
11 and 12
december 1975
chicago symphony

schumann symphony 3/perischetti symphony for strings/berlioz orchestral extracts from roméo et juliette

brooklyn
13 december 1975
chicago symphony

programme as for 11 and 12 december

washington
14 december 1975
chicago symphony

programme as for 11 and 12 december

new york
17 december 1975
chicago symphony

programme as for 4, 5 and 6 december

philadelphia
18 december 1975
chicago symphony

programme as for 11 and 12 december

new york
19 december 1975
chicago symphony

programme as for 11 and 12 december

vienna
5 and 7 january 1976
vienna symphony
wiener singverein

hindemith mathis der maler symphony/rossini stabat mater
arroyo/fassbänder/luchetti/arié

vienna
21 and 22
january 1976
vienna symphony

beethoven egmont overture/mozart violin concerto 5/mussorgsky khovantschina prelude/ mussorgsky-ravel pictures at an exhibition

tour of switzerland by vienna symphony orchestra

bern　　　　　　　　　　beethoven egmont overture/hindemith mathis der
23 january 1976　　　　maler symphony/mussorgsky-ravel pictures at an
vienna symphony　　　　　exhibition

geneva　　　　　　　　　*programme as for 23 january*
24 january 1976
vienna symphony

basel　　　　　　　　　　*programme as for 23 january*
25 january 1976
vienna symphony

zürich　　　　　　　　　*programme as for 23 january*
26 january 1976
vienna symphony

lausanne　　　　　　　　*programme as for 23 january*
27 january 1976
vienna symphony

vienna　　　　　　　　　blacher poem for orchestra/ravel piano concerto in g/
31 january and　　　　　schumann symphony 3
1 and 2 february 1976　*buchbinder, piano*
vienna symphony

berlin　　　　　　　　　schumann das paradies und die peri
25 and 26　　　　　　　 *donath/finnilä/schreier/brendel/miyahara*
february 1976
berlin philharmonic
ernst-senff-chor

berlin　　　　　　　　　haydn symphony 94/mahler symphony 1
29 february and
1 march 1976
berlin philharmonic

chicago
18, 19 and 20
march 1976
chicago symphony

webern 6 pieces op 6/mozart piano concerto 25/
mussorgsky-ravel pictures at an exhibition
alexeyev, piano

milwaukee
22 march 1976
chicago symphony

prokofiev symphony 1/mozart piano concerto 25/
mussorgsky-ravel pictures at an exhibition
alexeyev, piano

chicago
25, 26, 27 and
29 march 1976
chicago symphony
orchestra and chorus

beethoven programme
egmont overture/symphony 9
robinson/carlson/little/michalski

milwaukee
1 april 1976
chicago symphony

mahler symphony 9

chicago
2 april 1976
chicago symphony

programme as for 1 april

london
27 april 1976
london philharmonic

mozart symphony 39/bruckner symphony 9

vienna
5, 6, 7 and 8 may 1976
vienna symphony

mozart sinfonia concertante for wind/schubert
symphony 8

vienna
22 and 23 may 1976
vienna symphony

mozart symphony 39/bruckner symphony 9

vienna
19 and 20 june 1976
vienna symphony
wiener singverein

schumann das paradies und die peri
moser/finnilä/hollweg/krause

edinburgh haydn symphony 94/mahler das lied von der erde
26 august 1976 *hamari/mitchinson*
london philharmonic

edinburgh beethoven missa solemnis
28 and 29 *moser/reynolds/tear/howell*
august 1976
london philharmonic
edinburgh festival chorus

berlin *beethoven programme*
5 and 6 egmont overture/piano concerto 5/symphony 7
september 1976 *weissenberg, piano*
berlin philharmonic

linz webern 6 pieces op 6/beethoven piano concerto 4/
1 october 1976 schubert symphony 4
vienna symphony *buchbinder, piano*

tour of spain by vienna symphony orchestra
valencia webern 6 pieces op 6/beethoven piano concerto 4/
3 october 1976 schubert symphony 9
vienna symphony *buchbinder, piano*

valencia *brahms programme*
4 october 1976 piano concerto 1/symphony 4
vienna symphony *orozco, piano*

madrid *programme as for 4 october*
5 october 1976
vienna symphony

madrid *programme as for 3 october*
6 october 1976
vienna symphony

barcelona
7 october 1976
vienna symphony

programme as for 3 october

barcelona
8 october 1976
vienna symphony

programme as for 4 october

bratislava
9 october 1976
vienna symphony

programme as for 4 october

vienna
15, 16 and 17 october 1976
vienna symphony

programme as for 4 october

chicago
18, 19 and 20 november 1976
chicago symphony

bartok viola concerto/brahms symphony 1
preves, piano

milwaukee
22 november 1976
chicago symphony

programme as for 18, 19 and 20 november

chicago
24, 26 and 28 november 1976
chicago symphony

mozart violin concerto 4/bruckner symphony 9
perlman, violin

chicago
29 november 1976
chicago symphony

brahms programme
violin concerto/symphony 1
perlman, violin

ames
3 december 1976
chicago symphony

programme as for 18, 19 and 20 november

ames　　　　　　　　　　mozart symphony 41/bruckner symphony 9
4 december 1976
chicago symphony

vienna　　　　　　　　　beethoven symphony 9
31 december 1976 and　　*ghazarian/reynolds/hollweg/ridderbusch*
1 january 1977
vienna symphony
wiener singakademie

berlin　　　　　　　　　*schubert programme*
12 and 13 january 1977　symphony 8/symphony 9
berlin philharmonic

berlin　　　　　　　　　webern 6 pieces op 6/beethoven piano concerto 4/
17 and 18 january 1977　mussorgsky-ravel pictures at an exhibition
berlin philharmonic　　　　*pollini, piano*

tour of west germany by vienna symphony orchestra
munich　　　　　　　　 beethoven piano concerto 5/schubert symphony 9
22 january 1977　　　　*buchbinder, piano*
vienna symphony

stuttgart　　　　　　　　beethoven piano concerto 4/schubert symphony 9
23 january 1977　　　　*buchbinder, piano*
vienna symphony

frankfurt　　　　　　　　beethoven piano concerto 5/debussy prélude a
24 january 1977　　　　l'apres-midi d'un faune/stravinsky firebird suite
vienna symphony　　　　　*buchbinder, piano*

duisburg　　　　　　　　*programme as for 22 january*
25 january 1977
vienna symphony

hamburg　　　　　　　　*programme as for 24 january*
26 january 1977
vienna symphony

vienna **28, 29 and 30** **january 1977** vienna symphony	weber freischütz overture/mendelssohn violin concerto/debussy prélude a l'apres-midi d'un faune/ stravinsky firebird suite *mintz, violin*
paris **23, 24 and 26** **february 1977** orchestre de paris	mozart symphony 35/ravel ma mere l'oye/ bruckner symphony 2
chicago **31 march and** **1 and 2 april 1977** chicago symphony	mozart sinfonia concertante for wind/dvorak symphony 9
milwaukee **4 april 1977** chicago symphony	*programme as for 31 march and 1 and 2 april*
evanston **5 april 1977** chicago symphony	mozart sinfonia concertante for wind/schubert symphony 9
chicago **7 and 8 april 1977** chicago symphony	webern 5 pieces op 10/britten serenade for tenor, horn and strings/brahms symphony 4 *tear/clevenger, horn*
chicago **14, 15 and 16** **april 1977** chicago symphony orchestra and chorus	bach concerti for 2, 3 and 4 pianos/stravinsky les noces *jaffe/jones/creech/silins*
london **5 may 1977** london philharmonic	beethoven violin concerto/bruckner symphony 2 *perlman, violin*
london **8 may 1977** london philharmonic	*beethoven programme* egmont overture/violin concerto/symphony 7 *perlman, violin*

london
12 may 1977
london philharmonic
orchestra and chorus

bach mass in b minor
armstrong/baker/tear/bailey

prague
3 and 4 june 1977
czech philharmonic
prague philharmonic
chorus

beethoven programme
egmont overture/symphony 9
bohacova/mrazova/spisar/svorc
choral movement of the symphony sung in czech

florence
**10, 11 and 12
june 1977**
maggio musicale
orchestra

beethoven symphony 7/brahms symphony 4

vienna
21 june 1977
vienna symphony

tchaikovsky symphony 2/mussorgsky-ravel
pictures at an exhibition

vienna
24 and 26 june 1977
vienna symphony
vienna opera chorus

verdi messa da requiem
ricciarelli/fassbänder/carreras/raimondi

linz
27 june 1977
vienna symphony
vienna opera chorus

programme as for 24 and 26 june

jerusalem
16 july 1977
israel philharmonic
tel aviv chorus

beethoven symphony 9
armstrong/zakai/vickers/carmeli

tel aviv
18 and 19 july 1977
israel philharmonic
tel aviv chorus

programme as for 16 july

edinburgh
22 and 23
august 1977
new philharmonia
edinburgh festival chorus

mozart programme
symphony 36/requiem
mathis/watts/tear/shirley-quirk

edinburgh
25 august 1977
new philharmonia

bruckner symphony 8

stockholm
17 and 18
september 1977
swedish radio orchestra

bruckner symphony 8

london
2 october 1977
philharmonia
orchestra and chorus

mozart sinfonia concertante for wind/beethoven
symphony 9
armstrong/hodgson/tear/shireley-quirk

milan
12, 13 and 14
october 1977
la scala orchestra
and chorus

mozart symphony 41/beethoven symphony 9
m.price/valentini-terrani/hollweg/shirley-quirk

rome
23 and 24 october 1977
santa cecilia orchestra

beethoven symphony 7/brahms symphony 4

vienna
6 november 1977
vienna symphony
vienna opera chorus

brahms ein deutsches requiem
armstrong/krause

chicago
10, 11 and 12
november 1977
chicago symphony

haydn symphony 94/schubert symphony 9

chicago
15 november 1977
chicago symphony

beethoven symphony 7/mussorgsky-ravel pictures at an exhibition

chicago
17, 18 and 20 november 1977
chicago symphony orchestra and chorus

mozart programme
symphony 36/requiem
cuccaro/carlson/cole/morris

milwaukee
21 november 1977
chicago symphony

beethoven symphony 7/mussorgsky khovantschina prelude/mussorgsky-ravel pictures at an exhibition

chicago
23, 25 and 26 november 1977
chicago symphony

beethoven programme
piano concerto 5/symphony 3
arrau, piano

chicago
28 november 1977
chicago symphony

brahms programme
piano concerto 2/symphony 1
barenboim, piano

vienna
31 december 1977 and 1 january 1978
vienna symphony
bratislava philharmonic chorus

beethoven symphony 9
ghazarian/lilowa/hollweg/nimsgern

berlin
8 and 10 january 1978
berlin philharmonic

ravel ma mere l'oye/ravel piano concerto for the left hand/debussy la mer
block, piano

berlin
13 and 14 january 1978
berlin philharmonic
ernst-senff-chor

beethoven missa solemnis
moser/hamari/schreier/ridderbusch

amsterdam **20 january 1978** concertgebouw orchestra	mozart symphony 40/bruckner symphony 9
den haag **21 january 1978** concertgebouw orchestra	*programme as for 20 january*
amsterdam **22 january 1978** concertgebouw orchestra	*programme as for 20 january*
amsterdam **25 and 26 january 1978** concertgebouw orchestra	salviucci introduzione passacaglia e finale/berlioz les nuits d'été/brahms symphony 1 *baker*
groningen **28 january 1978** concertgebouw orchestra	mozart symphony 40/brahms symphony 1
chicago **2, 3 and 4 march 1978** chicago symphony	schubert-webern 6 deutsche tänze/schubert symphony 8/brahms violin concerto *stern, violin*
milwaukee **6 march 1978** chicago symphony	schubert symphony 4/brahms violin concerto *stern, violin*
chicago **9, 10 and 11 march 1978** chicago symphony	gabrieli sonata pian e forte/gabrieli canzon a 4/ mozart piano concerto 24/dvorak symphony 8 *curzon, piano*
chicago **16, 17 and 18** **march 1978** chicago symphony	beethoven egmont overture/beethoven violin concerto/schubert symphony 4 *carmirelli, violin* *giulini's final appearances with chicago symphony orchestra*

barcelona *mozart programme*
28 march 1978 symphony 36/requiem
philharmonia *donath/hodgson/hollweg/rintzler*
orchestra and chorus

barcelona haydn symphony 94/beethoven symphony 9
29 march 1978 *donath/hodgson/hollweg/rintzler*
philharmonia
orchestra and chorus

berlin haydn symphony 99/von einem an die nachgeborenen
19 and 20 april 1978 *hamari/fischer-dieskau*
berlin philharmonic
ernst-senff-chor

rome *schubert programme*
29 and 30 april 1978 symphony 8/symphony 9
santa cecilia orchestra

paris messiaen offrandes oubliées/ravel piano concerto in g/
10 and 11 may 1978 beethoven symphony 7
orchestre de paris *rigutto, piano*

vienna rubin sonatine für orchester/mahler lieder eines
18, 19, 20 and fahrenden gesellen/beethoven symphony 7
21 may 1978 *hamari*
vienna symphony

graz *programme as for 18, 19, 20 and 21 may*
23 may 1978
vienna symphony

vienna *schubert programme*
27 and 28 may 1978 6 deutsche tänze/symphony 8/symphony 4
vienna symphony

vienna
24 and 25 june 1978
vienna symphony

bruckner symphony 8

florence
4 and 5 july 1978
maggio musicale
orchestra

schubert programme
symphony 8/symphony 9

edinburgh
20 august 1978
international youth
orchestra and chorus

mozart violin concerto 3/beethoven symphony 9
armstrong/watts/tear/rintzler/stern, violin

edinburgh
25 and 26 august 1978
london philharmonic
edinburgh festival chorus

brahms programme
tragic overture/ein deutsches requiem
cotrubas/fischer-dieskau

berlin
13 and 14
september 1978
berlin philharmonic
ernst-senff-chor

gabrieli sonata pian e forte/geminiani concerto
op 3 no 2/rossini stabat mater
stefan-savova/hamari/luchetti/raimondi

milan
11, 12 and 13
october 1978
la scala orchestra
vienna opera chorus

brahms programme
tragic overture/ein deutsches requiem
armstrong (donath)/krause

los angeles
26, 27, 28 and
october 1978
los angeles philharmonic
california university and
los angeles chorale

beethoven programme
egmont overture/symphony 9
neblett/carlson/tear/estes

los angeles *schubert programme*
1, 2 and 3 symphony 8/symphony 9
november 1978
los angeles philharmonic

santa ana *programme as for 1, 2 and 3 november*
4 november 1978
los angeles philharmonic

los angeles *programme as for 1, 2 and 3 november*
5 november 1978
los angeles philharmonic

los angeles beethoven piano concerto 4/mussorgsky-ravel
7 november 1978 pictures at an exhibition/weber freischütz overture
los angeles philharmonic *gilels, piano*

los angeles chopin piano concerto 1/dvorak symphony 9/
9 and 10 messiaen offrandes oubliées
november 1978 *zimerman, piano*
los angeles philharmonic

san diego weber freischütz overture/chopin andante spianato
11 november 1978 et grande polonaise/chopin piano concerto 2/
los angeles philharmonic dvorak symphony 9
zimerman, piano

los angeles messiaen offrandes oubliées/chopin andante
12 november 1978 spianato et grande polonaise/chopin piano
los angeles philharmonic concerto 2/dvorak symphony 9
zimerman, piano

san jose weber freischütz overture/schubert symphony 8/
15 november 1978 beethoven symphony 3
los angeles philharmonic

las vegas　　　　　　　*programme as for 15 november*
16 november 1978
los angeles philharmonic

denver　　　　　　　　*programme as for 15 november*
18 november 1978
los angeles philharmonic

denver　　　　　　　　dvorak symphony 9/mussorgsky-ravel pictures at
19 november 1978　　　an exhibition
los angeles philharmonic

tempe　　　　　　　　*programme as for 19 november*
21 november 1978
los angeles philharmonic

santa ana　　　　　　　*programme as for 19 november*
26 november 1978
los angeles philharmonic

santa barbara　　　　　*programme as for 15 november*
29 november 1978
los angeles philharmonic

palm springs　　　　　*programme as for 15 november*
30 november 1978
los angeles philharmonic

los angeles　　　　　　mozart serenade for 13 wind/stravinsky octet
2 december 1978
los angeles philharmonic

berlin　　　　　　　　mozart piano concerto 17/bruckner symphony 2
13 and 14 january 1979　*pollini, piano*
berlin philharmonic

amsterdam　　　　　　rossini semiramide overture/strauss violin concerto/
17, 18 and 19　　　　　mussorgsky-ravel pictures at an exhibition
january 1979　　　　　*krebbers, violin*
concertgebouw
orchestra

munich
25 and 26 january 1979
bavarian radio orchestra

haydn symphony 94/ravel ma mere l'oye/brahms symphony 1

vienna
31 january and
1 february 1979
vienna symphony

beethoven programme
piano concerto 3/piano concerto 5
michelangeli, piano

madrid
16, 17 and 18
february 1979
spanish national orchestra

beethoven programme
violin concerto/symphony 7
stern, violin

rome
25 and 26
february 1979
santa cecilia orchestra
and chorus

beethoven programme
egmont overture/symphony 9
armstrong/hamari/hollweg/moll

paris
8, 9 and 10 march 1979
orchestre de paris
and chorus

schubert symphony 4/rossini stabat mater
freni/valentini-terrani/luchetti/krause

los angeles
29 and 30 march 1979
los angeles philharmonic

mozart symphony 35/henze chaconne for violin and orchestra/brahms symphony 2
kremer, violin

santa ana
31 march 1979
los angeles philharmonic

programme as for 29 and 30 march

los angeles
1 april 1979
los angeles philharmonic

programme as for 29 and 30 march

palm springs **6 april 1979** los angeles philharmonic	mozart symphony 35/ravel piano concerto in g/ brahms symphony 2 *chung, piano*
san diego **7 april 1979** los angeles philharmonic	mozart symphony 35/hindemith mathis der maler symphony/brahms symphony 2
long beach **8 april 1979** los angeles philharmonic	*programme as for 7 april*
los angeles **12, 13, 14 and** **15 april 1979** los angeles philharmonic	weber freischütz overture/hindemith mathis der maler symphony/beethoven piano concerto 5 *eschenbach, piano*
los angeles **18 april 1979** los angeles philharmonic	mozart don giovanni overture/hindemith mathis der maler symphony/beethoven symphony 3
los angeles **19 and 20 april 1979** los angeles philharmonic	mozart don giovanni overture/mozart piano concerto 20/beethoven symphony 3 *serkin, piano*
san diego **21 april 1979** los angeles philharmonic	schubert symphony 8/beethoven symphony 3
los angeles **22 april 1979** los angeles philharmonic	*programme as for 19 and 20 april*
los angeles **26 and 27 april 1979** los angeles	debussy la mer/debussy prélude a l'apres-midi d'un faune/ravel shéhérazade/ravel ma mere l'oye *von stade*
santa ana **28 april 1979** los angeles philharmonic	*programme as for 26 and 27 april*

los angeles   *programme as for 26 and 27 april*
29 april 1979
los angeles philharmonic

new york   *beethoven programme*
2 and 3 may 1979   egmont overture/symphony 9
los angeles philharmonic   *robinson (neblett)/killebrew/tear/estes*
temple university choir

new york   *programme as for 26 and 27 april*
4 may 1979
los angeles philharmonic

new york   *programme as for 18 april*
5 may 1979
los angeles philharmonic

washington   weber freischütz overture/hindemith mathis der
6 may 1979   maler symphony/beethoven symphony 3
los angeles philharmonic

columbus   mozart symphony 35/hindemith mathis der maler
7 may 1979   symphony/beethoven symphony 3
los angeles philharmonic

chicago   mozart symphony 35/hindemith mathis der maler
9 may 1979   symphony/debussy prélude a l'apres-midi d'un
los angeles philharmonic   faune/debussy la mer

minneapolis   *programme as for 9 may*
10 may 1979
los angeles philharmonic

ames   *programme as for 6 may*
11 may 1979
los angeles philharmonic

ames
12 may 1979
los angeles philharmonic

ravel ma mere l'oye/ravel piano concerto in g/ debussy prélude a l'apres-midi d'un faune/debussy la mer
chung, piano

ames
13 may 1979
los angeles philharmonic

beethoven egmont overture/beethoven symphony 8/ mussorgsky-ravel pictures at an exhibition

ames
15 may 1979
los angeles philharmonic
iowa university choir

mozart programme
don giovanni overture/symphony 35/requiem
robinson/carlson/aler/howell

stockholm
1 june 1979
swedish radio orchestra and chorus

beethoven symphony 9
valjakka/finnilä/e.hagegard/haugland

brussels
7 june 1979
concertgebouw orchestra

webern 5 pieces op 10/mahler adagio from symphony 10/brahms symphony 4

amsterdam
9 june 1979
concertgebouw orchestra

programme as for 7 june

den haag
10 june 1979
concertgebouw orchestra

programme as for 7 june

vienna
24 june 1979
vienna symphony

mahler programme
adagio from symphony 10/das lied von der erde
fassbänder/jerusalem

florence beethoven symphony 9
30 june and *rinaldi/valentini-terrani/steinbach/nimsgern*
1 and 3 july 1979
maggio musicale
orchestra and chorus

vienna *beethoven programme*
21 september 1979 piano concerto 1/symphony 7
vienna symphony *michelangeli, piano*

vienna *mozart programme*
28 september 1979 symphony 40/requiem
vienna symphony *mathis/baltsa/schreier/holl*
vienna opera chorus

linz *programme as for 28 september*
29 september 1979
vienna symphony
vienna opera chorus

santa barbara mozart symphony 40/brahms symphony 1
11 october 1979
los angeles philharmonic

los angeles *programme as for 11 october*
12 october 1979
los angeles philharmonic

los angeles verdi messa da requiem
18 october 1979 *scotto/valentini-terrani/luchetti/talvela*
los angeles philharmonic
and master chorale

los angeles webern 5 pieces op 10/mozart sinfonia concertante
19 october 1979 for wind/dvorak symphony 7
los angeles philharmonic

los angeles
20 october 1979
los angeles philharmonic
and master chorale

programme as for 18 october

los angeles
21 october 1979
los angeles philharmonic

programme as for 19 october

los angeles
24 october 1979
los angeles philharmonic

gabrieli canzon a 8/gabrieli sonata pian e forte/
petrassi concerto for strings/saint-saens cello
concerto 1/ravel rapsodie espagnole
rothmuller, cello

los angeles
25 and 26
october 1979
los angeles philharmonic
and master chorale

programme as for 18 october

los angeles
27 and 28
october 1979
los angeles philharmonic

programme as for 24 october

los angeles
1, 2, 3 and 4
november 1979
los angeles philharmonic

mozart divertimento 11/beethoven piano concerto 4/
mahler adagio from symphony 10
arrau, piano

los angeles
7 november 1979
los angeles philharmonic

mozart divertimento 11/mozart piano concerto 24/
beethoven symphony 6
perahia, piano

los angeles
8, 9 and 10
november 1979
los angeles philharmonic

wagner tristan prelude and liebestod/mozart piano
concerto 24/beethoven symphony 6
perahia, piano

santa barbara
13 november 1979
los angeles philharmonic

ravel ma mere l'oye/chopin piano concerto 2/chopin andante spianato et grande polonaise/debussy la mer
zimerman, piano

san diego
17 november 1979
los angeles philharmonic

beethoven symphony 6/dvorak symphony 7

santa ana
18 november 1979
los angeles philharmonic

programme as for 17 november

washington
24 november 1979
los angeles philharmonic

webern 5 pieces op 10/mahler adagio from symphony 10/brahms symphony 1

boston
25 november 1979
los angeles philharmonic

programme as for 17 november

new york
26 november 1979
los angeles philharmonic

programme as for 17 november

new york
27 november 1979
los angeles philharmonic

programme as for 24 november

new york
28 november 1979
los angeles philharmonic
temple university choir

verdi messa da requiem
scotto/hamari/luchetti/talvela

cleveland
29 november 1979
los angeles philharmonic

beethoven symphony 6/brahms symphony 1

iowa
1 december 1979
los angeles philharmonic

programme as for 24 november

chicago
2 december 1979
los angeles philharmonic

programme as for 24 november

austin
3 december 1979
los angeles philharmonic

programme as for 24 november

houston
4 december 1979
los angeles philharmonic

programme as for 17 november

san antonio
5 december 1979
los angeles philharmonic

programme as for 17 november

santa ana
9 december 1979
los angeles philharmonic

mozart divertimento 11/wagner tristan prelude and liebestod/brahms symphony 1

los angeles
11 december 1979
los angeles philharmonic

beethoven egmont overture/beethoven violin concerto/brahms symphony 2
stern, violin

los angeles
13, 14, 15 and
16 december 1979
los angeles philharmonic

haydn symphony 95/serocki trombone concerto/schumann symphony 4
sauer, trombone

rome
20 and 21
january 1980
santa cecilia orchestra

brahms programme
violin concerto/symphony 1
milstein, violin

rome
23 january 1980
santa cecilia orchestra

beethoven symphony 2/brahms symphony 1

rome **27 and 28** **januarry 1980** santa cecilia orchestra and chorus	*brahms programme* tragic overture/ein deutsches requiem *armstrong/nimsgern*
bregenz **2 february 1980** vienna symphony	*beethoven programme* egmont overture/piano concerto 5/symphony 7 *leonskaja, piano*
los angeles **28 and 29 february** **and 2 march 1980** los angeles philharmonic	operatic overtures by rossini and verdi/rossini introduction theme and variations for clarinet and orchestra *zukovsky, clarinet*
los angeles **6 and 7 march 1980** los angeles philharmonic	schumann piano concerto/bruckner symphony 9 *lupu, piano*
san diego **8 march 1980** los angeles philharmonic	*programme as for 6 and 7 march*
los angeles **12, 13 and 14** **march 1980** los angeles philharmonic	brahms violin concerto/tchaikovsky symphony 6 *weiss, violin*
santa ana **15 march 1980** los angeles philharmonic	*programme as for 12, 13 and 14 march*
los angeles **16 march 1980** los angeles philharmonic	*programme as for 12, 13 and 14 march*

los angeles beethoven missa solemnis
3 and 4 april 1980 *putnam/connell/riegel/estes*
los angeles philharmonic
and master chorale

san diego brahms violin concerto/tchaikovsky symphony 6
5 april 1980 *dicterow, violin*
los angeles philharmonic

los angeles *programme as for 3 and 4 april*
6 april 1980
los angles philharmonic
and master chorale

santa barbara haydn symphony 99/mendelssohn violin
9 april 1980 concerto/tchaikovsky symphony 6
los angeles philharmonic *dicterow, violin*

los angeles haydn symphony 99/mendelssohn violin
10 and 11 april 1980 concerto/mozart symphony 41
los angeles philharmonic *dicterow, violin*

palm springs mozart symphony 40/tchaikovsky symphony 6
12 april 1980
los angeles philharmonic

los angeles *programme as for 10 and 11 april*
13 and 16 april 1980
los angeles philharmonic

los angeles beethoven symphony 2/brahms piano concerto 1
17 and 18 april 1980 *ashkenazy, piano*
los angeles philharmonic

santa ana *programme as for 17 and 18 april*
19 april 1980
los angeles philharmonic

los angeles   *programme as for 17 and 18 april*
20 april 1980
los angeles philharmonic

los angeles   franck psyché et éros/berlioz les nuits d'été/brahms
24, 25 and   symphony 1
26 april 1980   *baker*
los angeles philharmonic

los angeles   franck psyché et éros/berlioz les nuits d'été/
27 april 1980   beethoven symphony 3
los angeles philharmonic   *baker*

tour of europe by los angeles philharmonic orchestra
manchester   mahler adagio from symphony 10/beethoven
1 may 1980   symphony 3
los angeles philharmonic

london   *programme as for 1 may*
2 may 1980
los angeles philharmonic

vienna   mozart symphony 41/beethoven symphony 3
3 and 4 may 1980
los angeles philharmonic

linz   haydn symphony 99/beethoven symphony 2
5 may 1980
los angeles philharmonic

innsbruck   haydn symphony 99/ravel rapsodie espagnole/
6 may 1980   brahms symphony 1
los angeles philharmonic

zürich   *programme as for 1 may*
8 may 1980
los angeles philharmonic

strassburg beethoven symphony 2/tchaikovsky symphony 2
9 may 1980
los angeles philharmonic

freiburg *beethoven programme*
10 may 1980 symphony 2/symphony 3
los angeles philharmonic

bonn *programme as for 6 may*
11 may 1980
los angeles philharmonic

frankfurt *programme as for 10 may*
12 may 1980
los angeles philharmonic

milan beethoven symphony 2/tchaikovsky symphony 6
14 may 1980
los angeles philharmonic

florence *programme as for 1 may*
15 may 1980
los angeles philharmonic

madrid mozart symphony 41/tchaikovsky symphony 6
17 may 1980
los angeles philharmonic

madrid *programme as for 10 may*
18 may 1980
los angeles philharmonic

barcelona *programme as for 6 may*
19 and 20 may 1980
los angeles philharmonic

paris *programme as for 6 may*
22 may 1980
los angeles philharmonic

brussels *programme as for 10 may*
23 may 1980
los angeles philharmonic

london *programme as for 17 may*
25 may 1980
los angeles philharmonic

vienna mozart piano concerto 9/bruckner symphony 9
21 and 22 june 1980 *leonskaja, piano*
vienna symphony

hollywood bowl mozart le nozze di figaro overture/mozart
22 july 1980 symphony 41/verdi 4 pezzi sacri
los angeles philharmonic
and master chorale

hollywood bowl *beethoven programme*
1 and 2 august 1980 symphony 8/symphony 9
los angeles philharmonic *mitchell/carlson/mccoy/plishka*
and master chorale

hollywood bowl flute concerti by mozart and vivaldi/schubert
21 august 1980 symphony 9
los angeles philharmonic *rampal, flute*

santa barbara verdi forza del destino overture/haydn symphony 94/
15 october 1980 copland quiet city/brahms symphony 2
los angeles philharmonic

los angeles tchaikovsky symphony 6/verdi la traviata preludes/
18 october 1980 verdi vespri siciliani overture
los angeles philharmonic

los angeles **23, 24, 25 and** **26 october 1980** los angeles philharmonic	schumann symphony 3/mozart piano concerto 23/ beethoven symphony 7 *curzon, piano*
los angeles **29 october 1980** los angeles philharmonic	schumann manfred overture/schumann violin concerto/beethoven symphony 7 *kremer, violin*
los angeles **30 and 31 october 1980** los angeles philharmonic	*schumann programme* manfred overture/violin concerto/symphony 3 *kremer, violin*
santa ana **1 november 1980** los angeles philharmonic	*programme as for 29 october*
los angeles **2 november 1980** los angeles philharmonic	*programme as for 30 and 31 october*
los angeles **6, 7 and 9** **november 1980** los angeles philharmonic	haydn symphony 94/mahler das lied von der erde *troyanos/hofmann*
los angeles **12 november 1980** los angeles philharmonic	bizet l'arlésienne excerpts/operatic arias by bizet, donizetti, halévy, handel and verdi/overtures by cimarosa, rossini and verdi *domingo*
pittsburgh **19 november 1980** los angeles philharmonic	verdi vespri siciliani overture/william schuman symphony 3/tchaikovsky symphony 6
philadelphia **20 november 1980** los angeles philharmonic	*programme as for 19 november*
new york **21 november 1980** los angeles philharmonic	*programme as for 19 november*

ann arbor　　　　　　　　*programme as for 15 october*
23 november 1980
los angeles philharmonic

bloomington　　　　　　*programme as for 15 october*
24 november 1980
los angeles philharmonic

madison　　　　　　　　*programme as for 15 october*
25 november 1980
los angeles philharmonic

saint louis　　　　　　　*programme as for 15 october*
26 november 1980
los angeles philharmonic

palm springs　　　　　　brahms symphony 2/verdi vespri siciliani and
5 december 1980　　　　forza del destino overtures/verdi la traviata preludes
los angeles philharmonic

santa ana　　　　　　　 verdi forza del destino overture/william schuman
6 december 1980　　　　symphony 3/brahms symphony 2
los angeles philharmonic

florence　　　　　　　　 beethoven missa solemnis
5, 7 and 8 july 1981　　　*daniels/finnilä/tear/nimsgern*
maggio musicale
orchestra and chorus

hollywood bowl　　　　 mozart eine kleine nachtmusik/dvorak cello concerto/
28 july 1981　　　　　　mussorgsky-ravel pictures at an exhibition
los angeles philharmonic　 *harrell, cello*

hollywood bowl　　　　 verdi messa da requiem
30 july 1981　　　　　　*mitchell/quivar/gedda/plishka*
los angeles philharmonic
and master chorale

hollywood bowl **13 august 1981** los angeles philharmonic	*brahms programme* violin concerto/symphony 1 *perlman, violin*
hollywood bowl **18 august 1981** los angeles philharmonic	britten young person's guide/debussy clarinet rhapsody/haydn sinfonia concertante/vaughan williams tuba concerto/vivaldi piccolo concerto in a minor/vivaldi 4-violin concerto in b minor
london **23 august 1981** philharmonia orchestra and chorus	haydn symphony 94/rossini stabat mater *ricciarelli/valentini-terrani/gonzalez/raimondi*
vienna **26 september 1981** vienna symphony vienna opera chorus	mozart symphony 36/schubert mass in e flat *popp/lipovsek/moser/tomaschek/berry*
linz **27 september 1981** vienna symphony vienna opera chorus	*programme as for 26 september*
santa barbara **17 october 1981** los angeles philharmonic	mozart symphony 36/weber bassoon concertino in f/beethoven symphony 5 *breidenthal, bassoon*
santa ana **18 october 1981** los angeles philharmonic	*programme as for 17 october*
los angeles **22 and 23** **october 1981** los angeles philharmonic and master chorale	laderman symphony for brass/weber bassoon concertino in f/haydn nelson mass *armstrong/carlson/mack/lawrence/breidenthal*

san diego
24 october 1981
los angeles philharmonic

laderman symphony for brass/weber bassoon concertino in f/beethoven symphony 5
breidenthal, bassoon

los angeles
25 october 1981
los angeles philharmonic and master chorale

programme as for 22 and 23 october

los angeles
28, 29 and 30 october 1981
los angeles philharmonic

mozart symphony 36/barber cello concerto/ beethoven symphony 5
rose, cello

santa ana
31 october 1981
los angeles philharmonic

hindemith concert music for brass and strings/ barber cello concerto/brahms symphony 1
rose, cello

los angeles
1 november 1981
los angeles philharmonic

programme as for 28, 29 and 30 october

los angeles
5 and 6 november 1981
los angeles philharmonic

hindemith concert music for brass and strings/ strauss 4 letzte lieder/brahms symphony 1
popp

san diego
7 november 1981
los angeles philharmonic

programme as for 5 and 6 november

los angeles
8 november 1981
los angeles philharmonic

programme as for 5 and 6 november

los angeles
11 november 1981
los angeles philharmonic

hindemith concert music for brass and strings/ beethoven piano concerto 2/brahms symphony 1
perahia, piano

los angeles beethoven piano concerto 2/bruckner symphony 7
12 and 13 *perahia, piano*
november 1981
los angeles philharmonic

santa ana mozart violin concerto 4/bruckner symphony 7
14 november 1981 *treger, violin*
los angeles philharmonic

los angeles *programme as for 12 and 13 november*
15 november 1981
los angeles philharmonic

santa barbara *programme as for 14 november*
18 november 1981
los angeles philharmonic

san diego *programme as for 14 november*
21 november 1981
los angeles philharmonic

berlin haydn symphony 104/hindemith concert music for
8 and 9 january 1982 brass and strings/brahms piano concerto 2
berlin philharmonic *weissenberg, piano*

berlin dvorak cello concerto/schubert symphony 9
10 and 11 february 1982 *borwitzky, cello*
berlin philharmonic

los angeles ravel ma mere l'oye/beethoven piano concerto 5/
11 and 12 march 1982 salviucci introduzione passacaglia e finale/
los angeles philharmonic stravinsky firebird suite
pollini, piano

santa ana ravel ma mere l'oye/haydn sinfonia concertante/
13 march 1982 salviucci introduzione passacaglia e finale/
los angeles philharmonic stravinsky firebird suite

los angeles *programme as for 11 and 12 march*
14 march 1982
los angeles philharmonic

los angeles verdi falstaff
13, 17, 19, 21, 24, *ricciarelli/boozer/hendricks/valentini-terrani/gonzalez/*
27 and 29 april *bruson/nucci*
and 1 may 1982
los angeles philharmonic
and master chorale

tour of japan by los angeles philharmonic orchestra
yokohama mozart symphony 36/bruckner symphony 7
7 may 1982
los angeles philharmonic

tokyo *programme as for 7 may*
13 may 1982
los angeles philharmonic

tokyo ravel ma mere l'oye/stravinsky firebird suite/
14 may 1982 brahms symphony 1
los angeles philharmonic

tokyo tchaikovsky symphony 6/verdi forza del destino
15 may 1982 overture/verdi la traviata preludes
los angeles philharmonic

yokohama mozart symphony 36/stravinsky firebird suite/
16 may 1982 beethoven symphony 5
los angeles philharmonic

mito *programme as for 16 may*
18 may 1982
los angeles philharmonic

matsudo *programme as for 15 may*
19 may 1982
los angeles philharmonic

nagoya *programme as for 14 may*
20 may 1982
los angeles philharmonic

osaka tchaikovsky symphony 6/beethoven symphony 5
21 may 1982
los angeles philharmonic

wakayama *programme as for 16 may*
23 may 1982
los angeles philharmonic

fukuoka *programme as for 14 may*
24 may 1982
los angeles philharmonic

london verdi falstaff
30 june and *ricciarelli/ boozer/ hendricks/ valentini-terrani/ gonzalez/*
3, 6, 9, 13 and *bruson/ nucci*
16 july 1982
covent garden
orchestra and chorus

london mozart symphony 36/bruckner symphony 7
19 july 1982
philharmonia

paris mozart symphony 36/verdi 4 pezzi sacri
22, 23 and 24
september 1982
orchestre de paris
and chorus

los angeles webern 6 pieces op 6/berg violin concerto/
14 and 15 october 1982 bruckner symphony 9
los angeles philharmonic *perlman, violin*

santa ana *programme as for 14 and 15 october*
16 october 1982
los angeles philharmonic

los angeles   *programme as for 14 and 15 october*
17 and 18 october 1982
los angeles philharmonic

los angeles   beethoven egmont overture/beethoven piano
21, 22, 23 and   concerto 4/dvorak symphony 8
24 october 1982   *perahia, piano*
los angeles philharmonic

los angeles   *brahms programme*
28, 29, 30 and   tragic overture/ein deutsches requiem
31 october 1982   *battle/nimsgern*
los angeles philharmonic
and master chorale

los angeles   laderman symphony for brass/haydn trumpet
3 november 1982   concerto/dvorak symphony 8
los angeles philharmonic   *stevens, trumpet*

los angeles   beethoven violin concerto/schubert symphony 4
4, 5 and 7   *milstein, violin*
november 1982
los angeles philharmonic

washington   verdi forza del destino overture/laderman
27 november 1982   symphony for brass/beethoven symphony 5
los angeles philharmonic

boston   schubert symphony 4/bruckner symphony 9
28 november 1982
los angeles philharmonic

portland   stravinsky firebird suite/haydn trumpet concerto/
29 november 1982   dvorak symphony 8
los angeles philharmonic   *stevens, trumpet*

greenvale   *programme as for 27 november*
30 november 1982
los angeles philharmonic

new york　　　　　　　　*brahms programme*
2 december 1982　　　　tragic overture/ein deutsches requiem
los angeles philharmonic　*battle/krause*
westminster choir

new york　　　　　　　　*programme as for 28 november*
3 december 1982
los angeles philharmonic

new york　　　　　　　　*programme as for 29 november*
5 december 1982
los angeles philharmonic

new york　　　　　　　　*programme as for 27 november*
6 december 1982
los angeles philharmonic

ann arbor　　　　　　　*programme as for 28 november*
7 december 1982
los angeles philharmonic

chicago　　　　　　　　*programme as for 27 november*
8 december 1982
los angeles philharmonic

dallas　　　　　　　　　*programme as for 28 november*
10 december 1982
los angeles philharmonic

florence　　　　　　　　bruckner symphony 9
31 december 1982 and
4 january 1983
maggio musicale
orchestra

florence　　　　　　　　verdi falstaff
16, 20, 23, 27 and　　*ricciarelli/boozer (di stasio)/gasdia (hendricks)/curry/*
30 january and　　　　*gonzalez/bruson/allen*
1 february 1983
maggio musicale
orchestra and chorus

rome *brahms programme*
13, 14 and 15 symphony 2/symphony 4
february 1983
santa cecilia orchestra

salisbury bruckner symphony 8
17 september 1983
philharmonia

london *programme as for 17 september*
18 september 1983
philharmonia

nottingham *programme as for 17 september*
19 september 1983
philharmonia

london *programme as for 17 september*
21 september 1983
philharmonia

milan *beethoven programme*
5, 6 and 7 october 1983 egmont overture/piano concerto 4/symphony 5
la scala orchestra *pollini, piano*

los angeles beethoven egmont overture/mozart piano
3, 4 and 6 concerto 23/brahms symphony 4
november 1983 *perahia, piano*
los angeles philharmonic

los angeles beethoven egmont overture/mozart sinfonia
12 november 1983 concertante for wind/brahms symphony 4
los angeles philharmonic

los angeles bruckner symphony 8
17, 18, 19 and
20 november 1983
los angeles philharmonic

rome
22, 23 and 24
january 1984
santa cecilia orchestra

schubert programme
symphony 4/symphony 9

berlin
11 and 12 february 1984
berlin philharmonic

bruckner symphony 8

berlin
14 and 15 february 1984
berlin philharmonic

schubert symphony 4/mahler das lied von der erde
fassbänder/araiza

los angeles
29 and 30 march
and 1 april 1984
los angeles philharmonic

schubert symphony 8/mahler das lied von der erde
quivar/vickers

san diego
4 april 1984
los angeles philharmonic

beethoven egmont overture/mozart sinfonia
concertante for wind/brahms symphony 4

santa barbara
6 april 1984
los angeles philharmonic

programme as for 4 april

los angeles
11 april 1984
los angeles philharmonic

programme as for 4 april

los angeles
12 and 13 april 1984
los angeles philharmonic

turchi adagio for orchestra/mozart piano
concerto 24/beethoven symphony 7
brendel, piano

santa ana
14 april 1984
los angeles philharmonic

programme as for 4 april

los angeles
15 april 1984
los angeles philharmonic

programme as for 12 and 13 april
giulini's final appearance with los angeles philharmonic and
final appearance in the united states

linz　　　　　　　　　　bruckner symphony 8
25 may 1984
vienna philharmonic

vienna　　　　　　　　　*programme as for 25 may*
26, 27 and 29 may 1984
vienna philharmonic

rome　　　　　　　　　　*programme as for 25 may*
3, 4 and 5 june 1984
santa cecilia orchestra

florence　　　　　　　　*beethoven programme*
29 and 30 june 1984　　egmont overture/piano concerto 4/symphony 7
maggio musicale　　　　　　*perahia, piano*
orchestra

london　　　　　　　　　*brahms programme*
23 and 25　　　　　　　tragic overture/ein deutsches requiem
september 1984　　　　　*battle/nimsgern*
philharmonia
orchestra and chorus

london　　　　　　　　　*brahms programme*
28 september 1984　　　symphony 2/symphony 4
philharmonia

cardiff　　　　　　　　　*programme as for 28 september*
29 september 1984
philharmonia

london　　　　　　　　　*brahms programme*
1 and 2 october 1984　　symphony 3/symphony 1
philharmonia

milan　　　　　　　　　　*programme as for 28 september*
24, 25 and 26
october 1984
la scala orchestra

rome
24, 25, 26 and
27 november 1984
santa cecilia
orchestra and chorus

mozart programme
symphony 39/requiem
coburn/quivar/winbergh/macurdy

milan
9 december 1984
la scala philharmonic

brahms programme
symphony 3/symphony 1

ravenna
10 december 1984
la scala philharmonic

programme as for 9 december

paris
6, 7 and 8
february 1985
orchestre de paris

brahms programme
symphony 2/symphony 4

berlin
2 and 3 march 1985
berlin philharmonic
ernst-senff-chor

mozart programme
symphony 39/requiem
marshall/gjevang/wohlers/ramey

berlin
5 and 6 march 1985
berlin philharmonic

mozart piano concerto 23/bruckner symphony 7
perahia, piano

florence
17, 19, 20 and
21 march 1985
maggio musicale
orchestra and chorus

brahms ein deutsches requiem
hendricks/weikl

cardiff
12 may 1985
philharmonia
orchestra and chorus

beethoven missa solemnis
harwood/hodgson/jerusalem/lloyd

london
14 and 16 may 1985
philharmonia
orchestra and chorus

programme as for 12 may

brighton *programme as for 12 may*
17 may 1985
philharmonia
orchestra and chorus

rome *beethoven programme*
1, 2, 3 and 4 piano concerto 4/symphony 5
june 1985 *perahia, piano*
santa cecilia orchestra

florence bach mass in b minor
28 june 1985 *hendricks/quivar/tear/shirley-quirk*
maggio musicale
orchestra and chorus

lucca *programme as for 28 june*
29 june 1985
maggio musicale
orchestra and chorus

florence *programme as for 28 june*
30 june 1985
maggio musicale
orchestra and chorus

berlin bach mass in b minor
13 and 14 *popp/soffel/araiza/nimsgern*
september 1985
berlin philharmonic
ernst-senff-chor

parma *brahms programme*
29 september 1985 symphony 2/symphony 4
la scala philharmonic

regio emilia *programme as for 29 september*
1 october 1985
la scala philharmonic

ravenna *programme as for 29 september*
6 october 1985
la scala philharmonic

modena *programme as for 29 september*
8 october 1985
la scala philharmonic

bolzano *programme as for 29 september*
12 october 1985
la scala philharmonic

rome beethoven missa solemnis
20, 21 and 22 *donath/ soffel/ protschka/ sotin*
october 1985
santa cecilia
orchestra and chorus

milan beethoven violin concerto/schumann symphony 3
26, 27 and 28 *accardo, violin*
october 1985
la scala orchestra

london bach mass in b minor
17 and 18 *nicolesco/ rigby/ tear/ luxon*
november 1985
philharmonia
orchestra and chorus

london *beethoven programme*
21 and 22 egmont overture/violin concerto/symphony 5
november 1985 *accardo, violin*
philharmonia

nottingham *programme as for 21 and 22 november*
23 november 1985
philharmonia

stockholm bruckner symphony 8
8 december 1985
world philharmonic

trieste
6 january 1986
la scala philharmonic

brahms programme
symphony 2/symphony 4

munich
15, 16 and 18 january 1986
munich philharmonic

bruckner symphony 8

berlin
4 and 5 february 1986
berlin philharmonic

schumann programme
manfred overture/violin concerto/symphony 3
kremer, violin

berlin
8 and 9 february 1986
berlin philharmonic
ernst-senff-chor

franck symphony in d minor/fauré requiem
hendricks/desderi

milan
24 february 1986
la scala philharmonic

franck symphony in d minor/mussorgsky-ravel pictures at an exhibition

cardiff
8 march 1986
philharmonia orchestra and chorus

franck symphony in d minor/fauré requiem
battle/schmidt

london
9 march 1986
philharmonia orchestra and chorus

programme as for 8 march

reading
10 march 1986
philharmonia orchestra and chorus

programme as for 8 march

london
11 march 1986
philharmonia orchestra and chorus

programme as for 8 march

munich
27 and 28 march 1986
munich philharmonic
orchestra and chorus

beethoven missa solemnis
donath/fassbänder/araiza/dean

paris
9, 10 and 11 april 1986
orchestre de paris
and chorus

schubert symphony 8/fauré requiem
hendricks/hagegard

milan
21 april 1986
la scala philharmonic

schubert programme
symphony 4/symphony 9

lugano
25 april 1986
la scala philharmonic

programme as for 21 april

rome
4, 5 and 6 may 1986
santa cecilia orchestra

schubert symphony 8/mahler das lied von der erde
fassbänder/araiza

milan
11 may 1986
la scala orchestra
and chorus

beethoven symphony 9
mattila/valentini-terrani/araiza/weikl

bergamo
18 may 1986
la scala philharmonic

schubert symphony 4/brahms symphony 4

vienna
7, 8 and 10 june 1986
vienna philharmonic

haydn symphony 99/bruckner symphony 7

piacenza
15 june 1986
la scala philharmonic

brahms programme
symphony 3/symphony 1

berlin
9 and 10 september 1986
berlin philharmonic
ernst-senff-chor

verdi messa da requiem
varady/quivar/cole/dean

milan
24, 25, 26 and
27 september 1986
la scala orchestra
and chorus

beethoven missa solemnis
hendricks/ gjevang/ protschka/ holl

cremona
4 october 1986
la scala philharmonic

schubert symphony 8/brahms symphony 1

madrid
11 october 1986
la scala philharmonic

programme as 4 october

florence
26 october 1986
la scala philharmonic

schubert symphony 8/brahms symphony 4

london
9 and 11 november 1986
philharmonia
orchestra and chorus

verdi messa da requiem
roark-strummer/ quivar/ davies/ burchuladze

munich
11, 12, 13 and
15 december 1986
munich philharmonic

schubert symphony 8/mahler das lied von der erde
fassbänder/ araiza

rome
3, 4, 5 and 6
january 1987
santa cecilia orchestra

brahms programme
symphony 3/symphony 4

florence
11, 12, 14 and
15 february 1987
maggio musicale
orchestra and chorus

beethoven missa solemnis
connell/ soffel/ laubenthal/ sotin

milan
23 february 1987
la scala philharmonic

mozart programme
symphony 39/symphony 40

milan
20 march 1987
la scala philharmonic

tchaikovsky symphony 2/dvorak symphony 8

salzburg
12 and 18 april 1987
berlin philharmonic

bruckner symphony 8

lugano
25 april 1987
la scala philharmonic

mozart symphony 39/brahms symphony 4

milan
28 april 1987
la scala orchestra
and chorus

schubert symphony 8/verdi va pensiero from nabucco

bergamo
5 may 1987
la scala philharmonic

brahms programme
piano concerto 2/symphony 2
oppitz, piano

rome
10, 11 and 12 may 1987
santa cecilia
orchestra and chorus

bach mass in b minor
ameling/otter/moser/schmidt

brescia
18 may 1987
la scala philharmonic

brahms programme
piano concerto 1/symphony 4
oppitz, piano

florence
24 and 27 may 1987
maggio musicale
orchestra

schubert symphony 4/schumann symphony 3

vienna
20, 21 and 22 june 1987
vienna philharmonic
vienna opera chorus

brahms ein deutsches requiem
bonney/schmidt

linz
23 june 1987
vienna philharmonic
vienna opera chorus

programme as for 20, 21 and 22 june

salzburg
2 august 1987
vienna philharmonic

mozart symphony 40/mahler das lied von der erde
fassbänder/araiza

berlin
**9 and 10
september 1987**
berlin philharmonic
ernst-senff-chor

schubert programme
symphony 4/mass in e flat
popp/soffel/k.lewis/lavender/schmidt

varese
13 september 1987
la scala philharmonic

schubert symphony 8/brahms symphony 4

stresa
18 september 1987
la scala philharmonic

programme as for 13 september

gstaad
19 september 1987
la scala philharmonic

programme as for 13 september

cremona
28 september 1987
la scala philharmonic

brahms programme
violin concerto/symphony 4
accardo, violin

munich
20 and 21 october 1987
munich philharmonic
orchestra and chorus

brahms ein deutsches requiem
hendricks/weikl

milan
4, 5 and 6
november 1987
la scala orchestra

bruckner symphony 9

bergamo
11 november 1987
la scala philharmonic

bruckner symphony 9

cardiff
19 november 1987
philharmonia
orchestra and chorus

mozart programme
symphony 39/requiem
harwood/gjevang/seiffert/lloyd

london
22 and 23
november 1987
philharmonia
orchestra and chorus

programme as for 21 november

london
18 and 20
december 1987
philharmonia

schumann programme
manfred overture/piano concerto/symphony 3
lupu, piano

paris
6, 7 and 8
january 1988
orchestre de paris
and chorus

bach mass in b minor
bonney/van nes/k.lewis/gilfry

florence
8, 9 and 10 march 1988
maggio musicale
orchestra and chorus

franck symphony in d minor/fauré requiem
laki/duesing

pistoia
11 march 1988
maggio musicale
orchestra and chorus

programme as for 8, 9 and 10 march

florence
12 and 13 march 1988
maggio musicale
orchestra and chorus

programme as for 8, 9 and 10 march

lugano
11 april 1988
la scala philharmonic

beethoven symphony 6/brahms symphony 2

berlin
21 april 1988
berlin philharmonic

brahms programme
symphony 2/symphony 4

berlin
24 april 1988
berlin philharmonic

mozart sinfonia concertante for wind/brahms symphony 1

zürich
2 may 1988
la scala philharmonic

schubert symphony 8/brahms symphony 4

rome
15, 16 and 17 may 1988
santa cecilia orchestra

bruckner symphony 9

napoli
23 may 1988
la scala philharmonic

beethoven violin concerto/brahms symphony 4
accardo, violin

milan
30 may 1988
la scala philharmonic

beethoven symphony 6/brahms symphony 4

vienna
10, 11 and 12 june 1988
vienna philharmonic

bruckner symphony 9

berlin
10 and 11
september 1988
berlin philharmonic
ernst-senff-chor

brahms ein deutsches requiem
bonney/schmidt

rome
1, 2, 3 and 4
october 1988
santa cecilia orchestra

beethoven symphony 6/brahms symphony 1

milan
26, 27 and 28
october 1988
la scala orchestra

schubert symphony 4/mahler das lied von der erde
fassbänder/araiza

verona
31 october 1988
la scala philharmonic

schubert symphony 8/brahms symphony 4

lucerne
6 november 1988
la scala philharmonic

schubert programme
symphony 4/symphony 9

amsterdam
23, 24 and 25
november 1988
concertgebouw
orchestra

schubert symphony 4/brahms symphony 4

munich
16, 17 and 18
december 1988
munich philharmonic

mozart piano concerto 12/bruckner symphony 7
pires, piano

paris   mozart symphony 40/bruckner symphony 7
18, 19 and 20
january 1989
orchestre de paris

berlin   beethoven symphony 9
15 and 16 february 1989   *varady/zimmermann/goldberg/lorenz*
berlin philharmonic
ernst-senff-chor

london   beethoven symphony 9
5 and 7 march 1989   *varady/zimmermann/k.lewis/howell*
philharmonia
orchestra and chorus

madrid   *programme as for 5 and 7 march*
18 march 1989
philharmonia
orchestra and chorus

barcelona   *programme as for 5 and 7 march*
19 march 1989
philharmonia
orchestra and chorus

turin   schubert symphony 4/brahms symphony 4
2 april 1989
turin philharmonic

lugano   schubert symphony 8/brahms symphony 1
6 april 1989
la scala philharmonic

london   *mozart programme*
18 and 20 april 1989   symphony 40/requiem
philharmonia   *dawson/von stade/blochwitz/estes*
orchestra and chorus

trieste
24 april 1989
la scala philharmonic

schumann cello concerto/brahms symphony 1
brunello, cello

milan
25 april 1989
la scala philharmonic

programme as for 6 april

milan
8 may 1989
la scala philharmonic

schumann cello concerto/bruckner symphony 7
brunello, cello

vienna
20, 21 and 24 may 1989
vienna philharmonic

haydn symphony 94/brahms symphony 4

ravenna
29 may 1989
la scala philharmonic

programme as for 8 may

rome
3, 4, 5 and 6 june 1989
santa cecilia
orchestra and chorus

beethoven symphony 9
popp/hamari/cole/sotin

florence
28 june 1989
maggio musicale
orchestra

brahms programme
symphony 3/symphony 1

florence
30 june 1989
maggio musicale
orchestra

brahms programme
symphony 2/symphony 4

salzburg
15 august 1989
vienna philharmonic

brahms programme
symphony 3/symphony 4

berlin
10 and 12
september 1989
berlin philharmonic

bruckner symphony 9
memorial concert for herbert von karajan; orchestra also played schubert symphony 8 without conductor

hamburg bruckner symphony 9
12 september 1989
berlin philharmonic

milan *brahms programme*
18, 19, 20 and symphony 3/symphony 4
21 september 1989
la scala orchestra

stockholm verdi messa da requiem
29 and 30 *sweet/malakova/k.lewis/furlanetto*
september 1989
swedish radio orchestra
and choirs

london weber freischütz overture/mendelssohn violin
26 and 29 october 1989 concerto/brahms symphony 1
philharmonia *accardo, violin*

amsterdam brahms symphony 3/ravel ma mere l'oye/
22, 23, 24 and stravinsky firebird suite
26 november 1989
concertgebouw
orchestra

paris haydn symphony 94/mahler das lied von der erde
6, 7 and 8 *van nes/k.lewis*
december 1989
orchestre de paris

toulouse schumann symphony 3/ravel ma mere l'oye/
15 january 1990 stravinsky firebird suite
la scala philharmonic

madrid *programme as for 15 january*
29 january 1990
la scala philharmonic

berlin
15 and 16 february 1990
berlin philharmonic

schumann symphony 3/mussorgsky-ravel pictures at an exhibition

london
4 march 1990
philharmonia

brahms symphony 3/ravel ma mere l'oye/ stravinsky firebird suite

warwick
5 march 1990
philharmonia

programme as for 4 march

london
7 march 1990
philharmonia

programme as for 4 march

paris
12 march 1990
la scala philharmonic

schubert symphony 8/brahms symphony 4

lugano
19 march 1990
la scala philharmonic

schumann symphony 3/ravel ma mere l'oye/ stravinsky firebird suite

lugano
26 march 1990
la scala philharmonic

franck symphony in d minor/musorgsky-ravel pictures at an exhibition

bologna
30 april and
14 may 1990
la scala philharmonic

programme as for 19 march

vienna
24, 26 and 27 may 1990
vienna philharmonic

brahms symphony 3/schumann symphony 3

florence
30 may 1990
maggio musicale
orchestra

schumann symphony 3/ravel ma mere l'oye/ stravinsky firebird suite

napoli *programme as for 19 march*
4 june 1990
la scala philharmonic

strassburg *programme as for 19 march*
11 june 1990
la scala philharmonic

milan *programme as for 19 march*
24 june 1990
la scala philharmonic

ravenna beethoven symphony 9
26 july 1990 *dessi/van nes/k.lewis/howell*
maggio musicale
orchestra and chorus

berlin verdi 4 pezzi sacri/beethoven symphony 6
7 and 8 september 1990 *sweet*
berlin philharmonic
ernst-senff-chor

montreux schumann symphony 1/brahms symphony 1
15 september 1990
la scala philharmonic

ludwigshafen *programme as for 15 september*
16 september 1990
la scala philharmonic

stresa *programme as for 19 march*
18 september 1990
la scala philharmonic

vienna beethoven symphony 9
29 and 30 *benackova/lipovsek (lilowa)/k.lewis (hollweg)/*
september 1990 *terfel (nimsgern)*
vienna symphony *giulini's final appearances with vienna symphony orchestra*
vienna opera chorus

milan
17, 18 and 19 october 1990
la scala orchestra
philharmonia chorus

bach mass in b minor
dawson/ manca di nissa/ k.lewis/ gilfry

zürich
28 october 1990
la scala philharmonic

brahms programme
symphony 1/symphony 4

lille
29 october 1990
la scala philharmonic

beethoven symphony 6/brahms symphony 1

madrid
5 november 1990
la scala philharmonic

beethoven programme
symphony 6/symphony 7

paris
14, 15 and 16 november 1990
orchestre de paris

schubert programme
symphony 4/symphony 9

valencia
26 november 1990
la scala philharmonic

programme as for 5 november

amsterdam
12, 13, 14 and 15 december 1990
concertgebouw orchestra

tchaikovsky symphony 2/dvorak symphony 8

rome
5, 6, 7 and 8 january 1991
santa cecilia orchestra

mozart programme
eine kleine nachtmusik/sinfonia concertante for wind/symphony 41

tenerife
13 january 1991
la scala philharmonic

programme as for 5 november 1990

las palmas *programme as for 5 november 1990*
14 january 1991
la scala philharmonic

toulouse mozart eine kleine nachtmusik/mozart flute
28 january 1991 concerto 2/beethoven symphony 7
la scala philharmonic *cavallo, flute*

milan *beethoven programme*
4 february 1991 violin concerto/symphony 7
la scala philharmonic *kremer, violin*

berlin *mozart programme*
13 and 14 february 1991 sinfonia concertante for wind/requiem
berlin philharmonic *margiono/van nes/heilmann/hale*
ernst-senff-chor

london *brahms programme*
7 march 1991 piano concerto 1/symphony 1
philharmonia *barenboim, piano*

london *brahms programme*
9 march 1991 symphony 3/symphony 1
philharmonia

london *programme as for 7 march*
10 march 1991
philharmonia

madrid *programme as for 9 march*
19 march 1991
philharmonia

valencia *programme as for 9 march*
20 march 1991
philharmonia

barcelona *programme as for 9 march*
21 march 1991
philharmonia

lisbon *programme as for 9 march*
22 march 1991
philharmonia

london *brahms programme*
5 may 1991 piano concerto 2/symphony 2
philharmonia *perahia, piano*

birmingham *programme as for 5 may*
6 may 1991
philharmonia

london *programme as for 5 may*
7 may 1991
philharmonia

paris *beethoven programme*
13 may 1991 symphony 6/symphony 7
la scala philharmonic

berlin *mozart programme*
23 and 26 may 1991 symphony 40/symphony 41
berlin philharmonic

strassburg mozart symphony 41/beethoven symphony 7
9 june 1991
la scala philharmonic

amsterdam *beethoven programme*
27 june 1991 symphony 6/symphony 7
concertgebouw
orchestra

cologne *programme as for 27 june*
28 june 1991
concertgebouw
orchestra

düsseldorf *programme as for 27 june*
29 june 1991
concertgebouw
orchestra

florence beethoven symphony 9
18 july 1991 *sweet/malakova/protschka/rydl*
maggio musicale
orchestra and chorus

siena *programme as for 18 july*
19 july 1991
maggio musicale
orchestra and chorus

salzburg mozart requiem
28 august 1991 *dawson/van nes/k.lewis/ramey*
vienna philharmonic *concert in salzburg cathedral*
vienna opera chorus

prague mozart symphony 41/beethoven symphony 7
7 september 1991
la scala philharmonic

berlin tchaikovsky symphony 2/ravel ma mere l'oye/
14 and 16 stravinsky firebird suite
september 1991
berlin philharmonic

montreux *beethoven programme*
21 september 1991 symphony 6/symphony 7
la scala philharmonic

brussels schubert symphony 8/brahms symphony 1
22 september 1991
la scala philharmonic

rotterdam *programme as for 22 september*
23 september 1991
la scala philharmonic

milan *beethoven programme*
25, 26 and 27 symphony 6/symphony 3
september 1991 *giulini's final appearances with the orchestra of la scala milan*
la scala orchestra

como *programme as for 7 september*
1 october 1991
la scala philharmonic

london verdi messa da requiem
6 october 1991 *sweet/malakova/cole/colombara*
philharmonia
orchestra and chorus

paris schumann symphony 3/ravel ma mere l'oye/
14 october 1991 stravinsky firebird suite
la scala philharmonic

tour of spain by philharmonia orchestra and chorus
valencia verdi messa da requiem
20 october 1991 *sweet (pollet)/malakova/cole/colombara*
philharmonia
orchestra and chotus

santander *programme as for 20 october*
21 october 1991
philharmonia
orchestra and chorus

barcelona *programme as for 20 october*
7 november 1991
philharmonia
orchestra and chorus

madrid *programme as for 20 october*
8 november 1991
philharmonia
orchestra and chorus

valencia *programme as for 20 october*
9 november 1991
philharmonia
orchestra and chorus

turin
24 november 1991
turin philharmonic

beethoven programme
symphony 6/symphony 7

vatican city
5 december 1991
rai roma orchestra
and chorus

mozart requiem
dawson/van nes/k.lewis/estes

rome
4 january 1992
santa cecilia orchestra

schubert programme
symphony 4/symphony 9

paris
**29 and 30 january
and 1 february 1992**
orchestre de paris
and chorus

verdi messa da requiem
pollet/malakova/winbergh/scandiuzzi

berlin
**20 and 22
february 1992**
berlin philharmonic

weber freischütz overture/mendelssohn violin
concerto/dvorak symphony 8
accardo, violin

milan
2 march 1992
la scala philharmonic

beethoven programme
symphony 8/symphony 3

berlin
18 and 19 march 1992
berlin philharmonic

mozart symphony 39/mahler das lied von der erde
fassbänder/k.lewis

milan
25 april 1992
la scala philharmonic

beethoven symphony 7

birmingham **26 april 1992** la scala philharmonic	*beethoven programme* symphony 8/symphony 3
london **27 april 1992** la scala philharmonic	*programme as for 26 april*
amsterdam **6 and 7 may 1992** concertgebouw orchestra	schumann piano concerto/dvorak symphony 9 *kissin, piano*
den haag **9 may 1992** concertgebouw orchestra	*programme as for 6 and 7 may*
vienna **23, 24 and** **25 may 1992** vienna philharmonic	schumann piano concerto/brahms symphony 1 *kissin, piano*
stockholm **12 and 13 june 1992** swedish radio orchestra	*brahms programme* symphony 3/symphony 4
luxembourg **10 august 1992** european union youth orchestra philharmonia chorus	beethoven symphony 9 *sweet/van nes/k.lewis/rootering*

copenhagen
12 august 1992
european union
youth orchestra
philharmonia chorus

programme as for 10 august

amsterdam
14 august 1992
european union
youth orchestra
philharmonia chorus

programme as for 10 august

lucerne
15 august 1992
european union
youth orchestra
philharmonia chorus

programme as for 10 august

munich
16 august 1992
european union
youth orchestra
philharmonia chorus

programme as for 10 august

berlin
13 and 14
september 1992
berlin philharmonic
ernst-senff-chor

verdi messa da requiem
sweet/quivar/cole/estes
giulini's final appearance with berlin philharmonic orchestra

monte carlo
19 september 1992
la scala philharmonic

beethoven programme
symphony 8/symphony 3

milan
23, 24 and 26
september 1992
la scala philharmonic

beethoven egmont overture/mendelssohn violin
concerto/beethoven symphony 3
vengerov, violin

london
2 and 4 october 1992
philharmonia

dvorak symphony 8/mussorgsky-ravel pictures at an exhibition

rome
18, 19 and 20 october 1992
santa cecilia orchestra and chorus

beethoven symphony 9
pollet/manca di nissa/k.lewis/stamm

paris
25, 26 and 27 november 1992
orchestre de paris

mozart eine kleine nachtmusik/mozart sinfonia concertante for wind/dvorak symphony 8

paris
28 november 1992
orchestre de paris

mozart eine kleine nachtmusik/dvorak symphony 8

genova
4 january 1993
la scala philharmonic

beethoven programme
symphony 4/symphony 3

vienna
21 january 1993
vienna philharmonic

weber freischütz overture
played at the vienna philharmonic ball

berlin
28 and 29 january 1993
staatskapelle berlin

dvorak symphony 7/mussorgsky-ravel pictures at an exhibition

amsterdam
10 and 11 february 1993
concertgebouw orchestra

programme as for 28 and 29 january

munich
27 and 28 february 1993
bavarian radio orchestra

schubert programme
symphony 4/symphony 9

london haydn symphony 94/britten serenade for tenor, horn
20 march 1993 and strings/dvorak symphony 9
philharmonia *k. lewis/ watkins, horn*

lisbon *beethoven programme*
25 april 1993 symphony 4/symphony 5
la scala philharmonic

santiago de compostela *programme as for 25 april*
26 april 1993
la scala philharmonic

milan brahms ein deutsches requiem
24 may 1993 *dawson/ schmidt*
la scala philharmonic
la scala chorus

vienna franck symphony in d minor/brahms symphony 2
10, 11 and 12 june 1993
vienna philharmonic

milan *beethoven programme*
20 june 1993 symphony 4/symphony 7
la scala philharmonic

verona *programme as for 25 april*
18 september 1993
la scala philharmonic

paris franck symphony in d minor/ravel ma mere l'oye/
6, 7 and 8 october 1993 debussy la mer
orchestre de paris

compiegne *programme as for 6, 7 and 8 october*
9 october 1993
orchestre de paris

rome
**30 and 31 october
and 1 and 2
november 1993**
santa cecilia orchestra

franck symphony in d minor/mussorgsky-ravel pictures at an exhibition

**florence
18, 19, 20 and
21 november 1993**
maggio musicale
orchestra

tchaikovsky symphony 2/mussorgsky-ravel pictures at an exhibition

**berlin
2 and 3 february 1994**
staatskapelle berlin

brahms programme
symphony 2/symphony 4

**milan
14 february 1994**
la scala philharmonic

ravel ma mere l'oye/ravel concerto for left hand/ franck variations symphoniques/debussy la mer
crossley, piano

**amsterdam
23, 24 and 25
february 1994**
concertgebouw
orchestra

franck symphony in d minor/ravel pavane pour une infante défunte/debussy la mer

**birmingham
25 march 1994**
philharmonia
orchestra and chorus

beethoven symphony 9
pollet/van nes/margison/miles

**london
26 march 1994**
philharmonia
orchestra and chorus

*programme as for 25 march
giulini's final appearance with the philharmonia orchestra*

**stockholm
15 and 16 april 1994**
swedish radio
orchestra and chorus

beethoven symphony 9
pollet/remmert/rolfe-johnson/miles

madrid
29 april 1994
la scala philharmonic

beethoven programme
symphony 4/symphony 7

madrid
30 april 1994
la scala philharmonic

franck symphony in d minor/ravel ma mere l'oye/
debussy la mer

vienna
15 and 17 may 1994
vienna philharmonic

beethoven programme
symphony 4/symphony 3

munich
1 and 2 june 1994
bavarian radio
orchestra and chorus

bach mass in b minor
ziesak/alexander/van nes/k.lewis/wilson-johnson

leningrad
23 june 1994
leningrad philharmonic

brahms programme
symphony 2/symphony 4

bolzano
16 august 1994
european union
youth orchestra

programme as for 23 june

salzburg
17 august 1994
european union
youth orchestra

programme as for 23 june

edinburgh
19 august 1994
european union
youth orchestra

programme as for 23 june

london
20 august 1994
european union
youth orchestra

programme as for 23 june

european tour by la scala philharmonic
leipzig   *beethoven programme*
4 september 1994   symphony 4/symphony 7
la scala philharmonic

dresden   schubert symphony 4/brahms symphony 1
5 september 1994
la scala philharmonic

montreux   *beethoven programme*
8 september 1994   symphony 4/symphony 5
la scala philharmonic

athens   *programme as for 8 september*
18 and 19
september 1994
la scala philharmonic

modena   *programme as for 8 september*
25 september 1994
la scala philharmonic

rome   mozart eine kleine nachtmusik/haydn sinfonia
4 october 1994   concertante/schumann symphony 3
santa cecilia orchestra   *giulini's eightieth birthday concert*

rome   bach mass in b minor
18, 19 and 20   *gasdia/ manca di nissa/ k.lewis/ pertusi*
december 1994
santa cecilia
orchestra and chorus

florence   *schubert programme*
3, 4 and 5   symphony 8/mass in e flat
february 1995   *ruffini/ sage/ ainsley/ bonfatti/ surjan*
maggio musicale
orchestra and chorus

paris
22, 23 and
25 march 1995
orchestre de paris
and chorus

haydn symphony 94/schubert mass in e flat
brown/malakova/ainsley/mikulas

munich
26 and 27 april 1995
bavarian radio
orchestra and chorus

schubert mass in e flat
ziesak/van nes/lippert/bünten/schmidt

rome
10, 11, 12 and
13 june 1995
santa cecilia
orchestra and chorus

schubert programme
symphony 8/mass in e flat
gavarini/f.caniglia/costantino/putelli/c.guelfi

padua
21 june 1995
la scala philharmonic

brahms programme
tragic overture/alto rhapsody/symphony 1
valentini-terrani

turin
26 july 1995
turin philharmonic

schubert symphony 8/brahms symphony 4

salzburg
30 january 1996
vienna philharmonic
arnold-schoenberg-chor

mozart requiem
mcnair/stutzmann/trost/miles

turin
15 and 16
february 1996
rai nazionale orchestra

bruckner symphony 9

ferrara
18 february 1996
rai nazionale orchestra

programme as for 15 and 16 february

amsterdam **13, 14 and** **15 march 1996** concertgebouw orchestra	*beethoven programme* symphony 4/symphony 5 *giulini's final appearance with concertgebouw orchestra*
munich **3 and 4 april 1996** bavarian radio orchestra	franck symphony in d minor/ravel ma mere l'oye/ debussy la mer
vienna **18 may 1996** vienna philharmonic vienna opera chorus	*bruckner programme* symphony 9/te deum *banse/kirchschlager/beczala/schubert* *concert in the vienna staatsoper; giulini's final appearance* *with the vienna philharmonic orchestra*
rome **9, 10 and 11 june 1996** santa cecilia orchestra	*schumann programme* piano concerto/symphony 3 *kissin, piano*
berlin **26 and 27 june 1996** staatskapelle berlin	schumann symphony 3/brahms symphony 4
kloster eberbach **29 june 1996** staatskapelle berlin	*programme as for 26 and 27 june*
stuttgart **18 and 20** **september 1996** sdr orchestra	bruckner symphony 9
caligari **18 and 19 october 1996** orchestra del teatro lirico di caligari	*brahms programme* symphony 3/symphony 4
rome **14, 17, 18 and** **19 november 1996** santa cecilia orchestra	*brahms programme* piano concerto 1/symphony 1 *zimerman, piano* *giulini's final appearances with santa cecilia orchestra*

dresden schubert symphony 4/brahms symphony 4
7 and 8 december 1996
dresdner philharmonie

paris *brahms programme*
8 and 9 january 1997 piano concerto 1/symphony 4
orchestre de paris *fleisher, piano*

florence brahms violin concerto/schubert symphony 4
14, 15 and 16 *vengerov, violin*
february 1997
maggio musicale
orchestra

caligari beethoven piano concerto 1/brahms symphony 2
15 and 16 march 1997 *pletnev, piano*
chamber orchestra
of europe

milan schubert symphony 4/brahms symphony 4
14 april 1997
la scala philharmonic

milan schubert symphony 8/brahms symphony 1
16, 17 and 19 *giulini's final appearances with la scala philharmonic orchestra*
april 1997
la scala philharmonic

ferrara mendelssohn violin concerto/schubert symphony 9
23 october 1997 *blacher, violin*
chamber orchestra
of europe

modena *programme as for 23 october*
24 october 1997
chamber orchestra
of europe

milan
26 october 1997
chamber orchestra
of europe

programme as for 23 october

lugano
28 october 1997
chamber orchestra
of europe

programme as for 23 october

turin
7, 9 and 10
january 1998
rai nazionale orchestra
chorus of orchestre
de paris

verdi messa da requiem
dragone/ lytting/ neill/ mikulas
giulini's final appearances with rai torino/ rai nazionale
orchestra

paris
28, 29 and
31 january 1998
orchestre de paris
and chorus

verdi messa da requiem
varady/ lytting/ neill/ mikulas
giulini's final appearances with orchestre de paris

florence
20, 21 and 22
march 1998
maggio musicale
orchestra

mozart symphony 41/brahms symphony 2
giulini's final appearances with maggio musicale orchestra

stockholm
24 and 25 april 1998
swedish radio orchestra
and choruses

beethoven missa solemnis
oelze/ groop/ elsner/ pape

valencia
19 may 1998
spanish youth orchestra

schubert symphony 4/brahms symphony 1

madrid *programme as for 19 may*
20 may 1998
spanish youth orchestra

baden-baden weber freischütz overture/saint-saens cello concerto 1/
1 july 1998 schubert symphony 9
sdr orchestra *maisky, cello*

zürich *programme as for 1 july*
3 july 1998
sdr orchestra

ROYAL FESTIVAL HALL
General Manager: T. E. Bean, C.B.E.

PHILHARMONIA CONCERT SOCIETY LTD.

Artistic Director:
WALTER LEGGE

presents

PHILHARMONIA ORCHESTRA

Leader: HUGH BEAN

Carlo Maria Giulini
Hans Richter-Haaser

BRAHMS

Tragic Overture, Op. 81
Piano Concerto No. 2 in B flat major, Op. 83
INTERVAL
Symphony No. 1 in C minor, Op. 68

Friday, May 16th, 1958
at 8 p.m.

Programme One Shilling

Management: IBBS & TILLETT LTD., 124 WIGMORE STREET, W.1

Photograph of Carlo Maria Giulini by Angus McBean

In accordance with the requirements of the London County Council—(i) the public may leave at the end of the performance or exhibition by all exit doors and such doors must at that time be open; (ii) all gangways, corridors, and external passageways intended for exit must be kept entirely free from obstruction, whether permanent or temporary; (iii) persons shall not be permitted to stand or sit in any of the gangways intersecting the seating, or to sit in any of the other gangways.

ROYAL FESTIVAL HALL
GENERAL MANAGER: T. E. BEAN, C.B.E.

PHILHARMONIA CONCERT SOCIETY LTD

ARTISTIC DIRECTOR:
WALTER LEGGE

PHILHARMONIA
ORCHESTRA
LEADER: HUGH BEAN

CARLO MARIA GIULINI
GYORGY CZIFFRA

ROSSINI: Overture, L'Italiana in Algeri
FRANCK: Symphonic Variations
WAGNER: Prelude and Liebestod from Tristan und Isolde

INTERVAL

LISZT: Hungarian Fantasia
MOUSSORGSKY-RAVEL: Pictures at an Exhibition

Thursday, 11th June, 1959
at 8 p.m.

Programme One Shilling

ROYAL FESTIVAL HALL
GENERAL MANAGER: T. E. BEAN, C.B.E.

PHILHARMONIA CONCERT SOCIETY LTD

ARTISTIC DIRECTOR:
WALTER LEGGE

PHILHARMONIA ORCHESTRA

LEADER: HUGH BEAN

CARLO MARIA GIULINI
ANDRÉ TCHAIKOWSKY

VERDI:	Overture, I Vespri Siciliani
DVOŘÁK:	Symphony No. 4 in G
	Interval
RACHMANINOV:	Rhapsody on a theme by Paganini
FALLA:	Suite, The Three-Cornered Hat

Monday, 25th April, at 8 p.m.

Programme One Shilling

ROYAL FESTIVAL HALL
General Manager: T. E. BEAN, C.B.E.

PHILHARMONIA CONCERT SOCIETY LTD

Artistic Director:
WALTER LEGGE

VERDI
MESSA DA REQUIEM

PHILHARMONIA ORCHESTRA & CHORUS

CARLO MARIA GIULINI

JOAN SUTHERLAND   FIORENZA COSSOTTO
LUIGI OTTOLINI   IVO VINCO

CHORUS MASTER: WILHELM PITZ

Sunday, June 12, 1960, at 7.30 p.m.

Programme One Shilling and Sixpence

ROYAL FESTIVAL HALL
General Manager: T. E. Bean, c.b.e.

PHILHARMONIA CONCERT SOCIETY Ltd

ARTISTIC DIRECTOR: WALTER LEGGE

PHILHARMONIA ORCHESTRA

LEADER: HUGH BEAN

MANUEL DE FALLA

Concerto for harpsichord and five solo instruments
La vida breve: Salud's Arias
Dance

Interval

El amor brujo
Suite No. 2 from 'The Three-cornered Hat'

TERESA BERGANZA
GEORGE MALCOLM
Harpsichord by Thomas Goff

CARLO MARIA GIULINI

Tuesday, January 16, 1962, at 8 p.m.

Programme One Shilling and Sixpence

ROYAL FESTIVAL HALL
General Manager: T. E. Bean, C.B.E.

PHILHARMONIA CONCERT SOCIETY Ltd

ARTISTIC DIRECTOR:
WALTER LEGGE

PHILHARMONIA ORCHESTRA

CARLO MARIA GIULINI

GEORGE MALCOLM	LIONEL SALTER
VIOLA TUNNARD	ROBERT KEYS

BACH	Concerto for Four Harpsichords
BRITTEN	The Young Person's Guide to the Orchestra
STRAVINSKY	Octet for Wind Instruments
RAVEL	Rapsodie Espagnole

Monday, April 16, 1962, at 8 p.m.

Programme One Shilling and Sixpence

ROYAL FESTIVAL HALL
General Manager: T. E. Bean, C.B.E.

PHILHARMONIA CONCERT SOCIETY LTD

ARTISTIC DIRECTOR:
WALTER LEGGE

PHILHARMONIA ORCHESTRA
LEADER: HUGH BEAN

CARLO MARIA GIULINI
HENRYK SZERYNG

WEBER	Overture, Der Freischütz
BRAHMS	Symphony No. 4 in E minor
SIBELIUS	Violin Concerto in D minor
DEBUSSY	La Mer

Tuesday, April 24, 1962, at 8 p.m.

Programme One Shilling and Sixpence

ROYAL FESTIVAL HALL

General Manager: T. E. Bean, C.B.E.

PHILHARMONIA CONCERT SOCIETY Ltd

ARTISTIC DIRECTOR:
WALTER LEGGE

CARLO MARIA GIULINI

MOZART: Eine kleine Nachtmusik, K.525
BRITTEN: Serenade for tenor, horn and strings

PETER PEARS   ALAN CIVIL

DEBUSSY: Two Nocturnes: Nuages and Fêtes

VERDI: Quattro Pezzi Sacri

JANET BAKER

PHILHARMONIA ORCHESTRA & CHORUS

CHORUS MASTER: WILHELM PITZ

Sunday, October 7, 1962, at 7.30 p.m.

Programme Two Shillings

ROYAL FESTIVAL HALL
General Manager: T. E. Bean, C.B.E.

PHILHARMONIA CONCERT SOCIETY Ltd
ARTISTIC DIRECTOR:
WALTER LEGGE

VERDI

Messa da Requiem

PHILHARMONIA ORCHESTRA AND CHORUS

PRINCIPAL CONDUCTOR: OTTO KLEMPERER
Leader: HUGH BEAN   Chorus Master: WILHELM PITZ

ELISABETH SCHWARZKOPF
CHRISTA LUDWIG
NICOLAI GEDDA
NICOLAI GHIAUROV

CARLO MARIA GIULINI

Sunday, June 23, 1963, at 7.30 p.m.

Programme Two Shillings

This concert is given in association with the Arts Council of Great Britain and the London County Council

ROYAL FESTIVAL HALL
General Manager: T. E. Bean, C.B.E.

PHILHARMONIA CONCERT SOCIETY Ltd

ARTISTIC DIRECTOR:
WALTER LEGGE

PHILHARMONIA ORCHESTRA

PRINCIPAL CONDUCTOR:
OTTO KLEMPERER

LEADER: HUGH BEAN

CARLO MARIA GIULINI
ARTUR RUBINSTEIN

BOCCHERINI: Symphony in C minor
MOZART: Piano Concerto in D minor, K.466

GRIEG: Piano Concerto in A minor
ROSSINI: Overture, Semiramide

Monday, November 25, 1963, at 8 p.m.

Programme One Shilling and Sixpence

This concert is given in association with the Arts Council of Great Britain and the London County Council

Royal Albert Hall
(Manager: Christopher Hopper)
Sunday, 6th December, 1964, at 7.30

VERDI Requiem

GIULINI New Philharmonia Orchestra
Leader: Hugh Bean

New Philharmonia Chorus
Chorus Master: Wilhelm Pitz

TERESA STICH-RANDALL
MARGA HÖFFGEN
RICHARD LEWIS
CARLO CAVA

In association with the Arts Council and the London County Council

Programme One Shilling and Sixpence

CARLO MARIA GIULINI

HAYDN
Symphony No 94
(The Surprise)

WAGNER
Five Wesendonklieder

VERDI
Four Sacred Pieces

Ingrid Bjoner

New Philharmonia Chorus
Chorus Master   Wilhelm Pitz

New Philharmonia Orchestra
Leader   Hugh Bean

ROYAL FESTIVAL HALL
General Manager John Denison CBE

Thursday 4 May 1967 at 8

Programme   Two Shillings and Sixpence

GIULINI

BRAHMS

Tragic Overture

Double Concerto

Symphony No. 1

Hugh Maguire

Jacqueline du Pré

New Philharmonia Orchestra
Leader Carlos Villa

ROYAL FESTIVAL HALL
General Manager John Denison CBE

Sunday 24 September at 7.30
Programme Two Shillings

GIULINI

FRANCK
Symphony in D minor

MOZART
Piano Concerto No. 21 in C K.467

CASELLA
La Giara

Rafael Orozco
Robert Tear

NEW PHILHARMONIA ORCHESTRA
Leader Carlos Villa

Royal Festival Hall (General Manager John Denison CBE)
Thursday 10 April 1969 at 8
Programme Two shillings

GIULINI

VERDI
Requiem

Gwyneth Jones
Josephine Veasey
Placido Domingo
Raffaele Arie

NEW PHILHARMONIA CHORUS
Chorus Master Wilhelm Pitz

NEW PHILHARMONIA ORCHESTRA
Leader Carlos Villa

Royal Festival Hall (General Manager John Denison CBE)
Tuesday 20 May 1969 at 8
Programme Two shillings and sixpence

Philharmonia Orchestra
Leader: Carl Pini

Philharmonia Chorus

Sunday 2 October 1977 at 7.30 pm

To mark the first season of the Philharmonia Orchestra and Philharmonia Chorus with their original titles restored, the Philharmonia Trust is delighted to present this Gala Concert which also celebrates the twentieth anniversary of the Chorus.

Carlo Maria Giulini

Gordon Hunt
John McCaw
Gwydion Brooke
Michael Thompson

Mozart: Sinfonia Concertante in E flat, K. 279b, for oboe, clarinet, bassoon and horn

Sheila Armstrong
Alfreda Hodgson
Robert Tear
John Shirley-Quirk

Beethoven: Symphony No. 9 (Choral)

Greater London Council
Royal Festival Hall
Director: George Mann OBE

Programme 25p

Philharmonia Orchestra

Patron: HRH The Prince of Wales
KG, KT, PC, GCB

Principal Conductor:
Giuseppe Sinopoli

Composer in Residence:
Oliver Knussen

Leader: Christopher Warren-Green

Co-Leader: Raymond Ovens

Sunday 23 &
Tuesday 25
September 1984
at 7.30

NB. There will be no interval during these performances.

Carlo Maria Giulini Brahms: Tragic Overture

Kathleen Battle
Siegmund Nimsgern
Philharmonia Chorus

Brahms: Ein deutsches Requiem

The Philharmonia Orchestra gratefully acknowledges the sponsorship of these concerts by

Nissan UK Limited

These concerts, promoted by Philharmonia Limited, are given with financial assistance from the London Orchestral Concert Board representing the Arts Council of Great Britain and the Greater London Council

Greater London Council
Royal Festival Hall

Programme 70p

Philharmonia Orchestra

Patron: HRH The Prince of Wales
KG, KT, PC, GCB

Principal Conductor:
Giuseppe Sinopoli

Composer in Residence:
Oliver Knussen

Leader: Christopher Warren-Green

Co-Leader: Raymond Ovens

Monday 1 &
Tuesday 2
October 1984
at 7.30

Carlo Maria Giulini

Brahms: Symphony No. 3

Brahms: Symphony No. 1

The Philharmonia Orchestra gratefully acknowledges the sponsorship of these concerts by

Nissan UK Limited NISSAN

These concerts, promoted by Philharmonia Limited, are given with financial assistance from the London Orchestral Concert Board representing the Arts Council of Great Britain and the Greater London Council

Greater London Council

Royal Festival Hall

Programme 70p

Philharmonia Orchestra

Patron: HRH The Prince of Wales
KG, KT, PC, GCB

Principal Conductor:
Giuseppe Sinopoli

Principal Guest Conductor:
Esa-Pekka Salonen

Composer in Residence:
Oliver Knussen

Leader: Christopher Warren-Green

Co-Leader: Raymond Ovens

Tuesday 14 &
Thursday 16
May 1985
at 7.30

Klemperer Centenary Concerts

Carlo Maria Giulini
Elizabeth Harwood
Alfreda Hodgson
Siegfried Jerusalem
Robert Lloyd
Philharmonia Chorus

Beethoven:
Missa Solemnis

The Philharmonia Orchestra gratefully acknowledges the sponsorship of these concerts by

THE CONDÉ NAST PUBLICATIONS

This concert, promoted by Philharmonia Limited, is given with financial assistance from the London Orchestral Concert Board representing the Arts Council of Great Britain and the Greater London Council

Greater London Council

Royal Festival Hall

Programme £1.00

Philharmonia Orchestra

Patron: HRH The Prince of Wales
KG, KT, PC, GCB

President: Vincent Meyer

Principal Conductor:
Giuseppe Sinopoli

Principal Guest Conductor:
Esa-Pekka Salonen

Composer in Residence:
Oliver Knussen

Leaders:
Christopher Warren-Green & Peter Thomas

**Carlo Maria Giulini
Mariana Nicolesco
Jean Rigby
Robert Tear
Benjamin Luxon
Philharmonia Chorus**
(Chorus Master: Horst Neumann)

Sunday 17 &
Monday 18
November 1985
at 7.30

These concerts, promoted by Philharmonia Limited, are given with financial assistance from the London Orchestral Concert Board representing the Arts Council of Great Britain and the Greater London Council

40th Anniversary Concerts

Bach: Mass in B minor

(NB. There will be no interval during these performances)

Sponsored by Nissan UK Limited

Greater London Council
Royal Festival Hall
Programme 80p

Philharmonia Orchestra

Sunday 9 & Tuesday 11 March 1986 at 7.30

Patron: HRH The Prince of Wales
KG, KT, PC, GCB

President: Vincent Meyer

Principal Conductor:
Giuseppe Sinopoli

Principal Guest Conductor:
Esa-Pekka Salonen

Composer in Residence:
Oliver Knussen

Leader: Peter Thomas

Carlo Maria Giulini   Franck: Symphony in D minor

Kathleen Battle   Fauré: Requiem
Andreas Schmidt
Philharmonia Chorus

The Philharmonia Orchestra gratefully acknowledges the sponsorship of these concerts by
THE CONDÉ NAST PUBLICATIONS LTD.

This concert, promoted by Philharmonia Limited, is given with financial assistance from the London Orchestral Concert Board representing the Arts Council of Great Britain and the Greater London Council

Greater London Council
Royal Festival Hall
Programme 80p

Philharmonia Orchestra

Patron: HRH The Prince of Wales
KG, KT, PC, GCB

President: Vincent Meyer

Principal Conductor:
Giuseppe Sinopoli

Principal Guest Conductor:
Esa-Pekka Salonen

Composer in Residence:
Oliver Knussen

Leader: Peter Thomas

Carlo Maria Giulini

**Linda Roark-Strummer
Florence Quivar
Arthur Davies
Paata Burchuladze
Philharmonia Chorus**

Sunday 9 &
Tuesday 11
November 1986
at 7.30

These concerts are promoted by
Philharmonia Limited, and are
Arts Council Funded.

Verdi: Requiem
(NB. There will be no interval during this performance)

Sponsored by Nissan UK Limited

Royal Festival Hall

Programme 80p

Philharmonia Orchestra

Sunday 22 & Monday 23 November 1987 at 7.30

Patron: HRH The Prince of Wales
KG, KT, PC, GCB

President: Vincent Meyer

Music Director:
Giuseppe Sinopoli

Principal Guest Conductor:
Esa-Pekka Salonen

Associate Conductor:
Owain Arwel Hughes

Composer in Residence:
Oliver Knussen

Leaders: Peter Thomas & Bradley Creswick

This concert is promoted by Philharmonia Limited, and is Arts Council Funded.

Carlo Maria Giulini

Elizabeth Harwood
Anne Gjevang
Peter Seiffert
Robert Lloyd
Philharmonia Chorus
(30th Anniversary Celebrations)

Mozart: Symphony No. 39

Mozart: Requiem

Sponsored by Nissan UK Limited

Royal Festival Hall

Programme £1.00

THE PHILHARMONIA

Patron: HRH The Prince of Wales KG, KT, PC, GCB
President: Vincent Meyer
Music Director: Giuseppe Sinopoli
Principal Guest Conductor: Esa-Pekka Salonen
Associate Conductor: Owain Arwel Hughes
Composer in Residence: Oliver Knussen
Leader: Bradley Creswick

SUNDAY 5 MARCH 1989 AT 7.30pm
Royal Festival Hall

CONDUCTOR: **CARLO MARIA GIULINI**

SOPRANO: **JULIA VARADY**

CONTRALTO: **MARGARITA ZIMMERMANN**

TENOR: **KEITH LEWIS**

BASS: **GWYNNE HOWELL**

THE PHILHARMONIA CHORUS

Beethoven: Symphony No. 9 'Choral'

Sponsored by

MITSUBISHI ELECTRIC (UK) LTD.

Programme £1.00

This concert is promoted by Philharmonia Limited,
and is Arts Council funded

THE PHILHARMONIA

Patron: HRH The Prince of Wales KG, KT, PC, GCB
President: Vincent Meyer
Music Director: Giuseppe Sinopoli
Principal Guest Conductor: Esa-Pekka Salonen
Associate Conductor: Owain Arwel Hughes
Composer in Residence: Oliver Knussen
Leader: Bradley Creswick

SUNDAY 29 OCTOBER 1989 AT 3.15pm
Royal Festival Hall

CONDUCTOR: **CARLO MARIA GIULINI**

VIOLIN: **SALVATORE ACCARDO**

Weber: Der Freischutz — Overture

Mendelssohn: Violin Concerto

Brahms: Symphony No. 4

Sponsored by
Mr. and Mrs. Sydney Lipworth

Programme £1.00

This concert is promoted by Philharmonia Limited,
and is Arts Council funded

THE PHILHARMONIA

Patron: HRH The Prince of Wales KG, KT, PC, GCB
President: Vincent Meyer
Music Director: Giuseppe Sinopoli
Principal Guest Conductor: Esa-Pekka Salonen
Composer in Residence: Oliver Knussen
Leader: Bradley Creswick

SUNDAY 4 MARCH 1990 AT 7.30pm
Royal Festival Hall

CONDUCTOR: **CARLO MARIA GIULINI**

Brahms: Symphony No. 3

Ravel: Mother Goose, Suite for Orchestra

Stravinsky: Suite, The Firebird (1919)

Sponsored by Nissan UK Limited

Programme £1.00

This concert is promoted by Philharmonia Limited,
and is Arts Council funded

orchestras conducted by carlo maria giulini

bavarian radio orchestra munich
boston symphony orchestra
chicago symphony orchestra
covent garden orchestra
dresdner philharmonie
hungarian state symphony
international youth orchestra
la scala orchestra milan
leningrad philharmonic orchestra
london symphony orchestra
maggio musicale orchestra florence
netherlands chamber orchestra
orchestra of hessischer rundfunk frankfurt
orchestra of teatro donizetti bergamo
orchestra of san carlo napoli
paris conservatoire orchestra
philadelphia orchestra
philharmonia orchestra london
known between 1964-1977 as new philharmonia orchestra
rai milano orchestra
rai torino orchestra
from 1994 forming basis of rai nazionale orchestra
rai roma orchestra
residentie orchestra den haag
royal philharmonic orchestra
spanish national orchestra
staatskapelle berlin
swiss festival orchestra
sometimes known as lucerne festival orchestra
turin philharmonic orchestra
vienna philharmonic orchestra
wdr orchestra cologne

berlin philharmonic orchestra
chamber orchestra of europe
concertgebouw orchestra amsterdam
czech philharmonic orchestra
european youth orchestra
israel philharmonic orchestra
la fenice orchestra venice
la scala philharmonic orchestra
london philharmonic orchestra
los angeles philharmonic orchestra
munich philharmonic orchestra
new york philharmonic orchestra
orchestra of teatro communale bologna
orchestra of teatro lirico caligari
orchestre de paris
pasdeloup orchestra paris
pittsburgh symphony orchestra

rai napoli orchestra

sdr orchestra stuttgart
rome opera orchestra
santa cecilia orchestra rome
spanish youth orchestra
tonhalle-orchester zürich

utrecht state orchestra
vienna symphony orchestra
world philharmonic orchestra

pianists who appeared with carlo maria giulini

alexeev, dimitri
arrau, claudio
bachauer, gina
brendel, alfred
bruins, theo
casadesus, robert
ciani, dino
crossley, paul
curzon, clifford
dichter, misha
firkusny, rudolf
fleisher, leon
frank, claude
gilels, emil
henkemans, hans
kempff, wilhelm
krainov, vladimir
lupu, radu
oppitz, gerhard
perahia, murray
pires, maria joao
richter-haaser, hans
roll, michael
salzman, pnina
scarpini, pietro
simon, abbey
tchaikovsky, andré
ts'ong, fou
watts, andré
zimerman, krystian
anda, geza
ashkenazy, vladimir
barenboim, daniel
browning, john
buchbinder, rudolf
chung, myung-whun
ciccolini, aldo
curzio, maria
cziffra, györgy
eschenbach, christoph
fischer, annie
foldes, andor
frantz, justus
haskil, clara
janis, byron
kissin, evgeny
leonskaja, elisabeth
malcuzynski, witold
orozco, rafael
pollini, maurizio
pletnev, mikhail
rogoff, ilam
rubinstein, artur
santoliquido, ornella
serkin, rudolf
solomon
tipo, maria
uninsky, alexander
weissenberg, alexis

violinists who appeared with carlo maria giulini
orchestra members who appeared in a solo capacity are not included

accardo, salvatore	blacher, kolja
chung, kyung-wha	de vito, gioconda
francescatti, zino	gimpel, bronislav
goldberg, szymon	gotkovsky, nell
grumiaux, arthur	gulli, franco
krebbers, hermann	kremer, gidon
magyar, thomas	martzy, johanna
menuhin, yehudi	milstein, natham
mintz, schlomo	oistrakh, david
oistrakh, igor	olof, theo
perlman, itzhak	schneiderhan, wolfgang
spivakov, vladimir	stern, isaac
szeryng, henryk	taschner, gerhard
ughi, uto	vengerov, maxim
wilkomirska, wanda	zukerman, pinchas

cellists who appeared with carlo maria giulini
orchestra members who appeared in a solo capacity are not included

amfiteatrof, massimo
du pré, jacqueline
harrell, lynn
mainardi, enrico
odnoposoff, ricccardo
rostropovich, msrislav
tortelier, paul

baldovino, amedeo
fournier, pierre
janigro, antonio
maisky, mischa
palm, siegfried
schafran, daniel

sopranos who appeared with carlo maria giulini
singers of minor operatic roles are not included

adani, mariella
ameling, elly
arroyo, martina
benackova, gabriela
bonney, barbara
borkh, inge
brouwenstijn, gré
carteri, rosanna
cerquetti, anita
cotrubas, ileana
daniels, barbara
de los angeles, victoria
dobbs, mattiwilda
dow, dorothy
fineschi, onelia
gasdia, cecilia
gayer, catherine
grümmer, elisabeth
hallin, margareta
harwood, elizabeth
hill, jenny
janowitz, gundula
jurinac, sena
kolassi, irma
laszlo, magda
maragliano, luisa
mathis, edith
mcnair, sylvia
mitchell, leona
molnar-talajic, liliana
neblett, carol
nicolesco, mariana
norman, jessye
pace, miti truccato
pashley, anne
pollet, francois
alexander, roberta
armstrong, sheila
battle, kathleen
bjoner, ingrid
boozer, brenda
bosabalian, luisa
callas, maria
cavalli, floriana
coburn, pamela
curtin, phyllis
dawson, lynne
de la bije, annette
donath, helen
dragoni, maria
freni, mirella
gatta, dora
ghazariam, sona
gulin, angeles
harper, heather
hendricks, barbara
hunter, rita
jones, gwyneth
kalmus, margherita
laki, kristina
lorengar, pilar
margiono, charlotte
mattila, karita
miljakovic, oliviera
moffo, anna
moser, edda
neway, patricia
noni, alda
oelze, christine
pagliughi, lisa
pobbe, marcella

290
sopranos who appeared with carlo maria giulini/concluded

popp, lucia
price, margaret
pütz, ruth-margret
ricciarelli, katia
rizzoli, bruna
ross, elinor
schwarzkopf, elisabeth
scotto, renata
shuard, amy
söderström, elisabeth
stadler, irmgard
steffek, hanny
sutherland, joan
tebaldi, renata
udovick, lucille
vaughan, elizabeth
vyvyan, jennifer
woytowicz, stefania
ziesak, ruth

price, leontyne
putnam, ashley
ratti, eugenia
rinaldi, margarita
roark-strummer, linda
sarocca, suzanne
sciutti, graziella
seefried, irmgard
sinclair, jeannette
stader, maria
stapp, olivia
stich-randall, teresa
sweet, sharon
tyler, marylin
varady, julia
vishnevskaya, galina
watson, claire
zareska, eugenia
zylis-gara, teresa

mezzo-sopranos and contraltos who appeared with carlo maria giulini
singers of minor operatic roles are not included

baker, janet
barbieri, fedora
boese, ursula
cadoni, fernanda
caniglia, flavia
connell, elizabeth
dinato, daniela
elmo, cloe
fassbänder, brigitte
gjevang, anne
guy, maureen
hesse, ruth
höffgen, marga
killebrew, gwendolyn
lilowa, margarita
ludwig, christa
malagu, stefania
meneguzzer, yolanda
orell, ester
pirazzini, miriam
radev, marianne
resnik, regina
rigby, jean
simionato, giulietta
soffel, doris
stutzmann, nathalie
valentini-terrani, licia
veasey, josephine
wagner, sieglinde
wilfert, herta
zimmermann, margarita

baltsa, agnes
berganza, teresa
bumbry, grace
canali, anna maria
carturan, gabriella
cossotto, fiorenza
dominguez, oralia
ericson, barbro
finnilä, birgit
gorr, rita
hamari, julia
hodgson, alfreda
hoffman, grace
kirchschlager, angelika
lipovsek, mariana
lytting, katya
malakova, petra
nicolai, elena
otter, anne sofie von
quivar, florence
remmert, birgit
reynolds, anna
rubio, consuelo
sinclair, monica
stade, frederica von
troyanos, tatiana
van nes, jard
verrett, shirley
watts, helen
zakai, mira
michelow, sybil

tenors who appeared with carlo maria giulini
singers of minor operatic roles are not included

ainsley, john mark
aler, john
alva, luigi
bergonzi, carlo
bottazzo, pietro
bünten, wolfgang
carreras, josé
cecchele, gianfranco
cole, vinson
costantino, ivano
del monaco, mario
duesing, dale
ercolani, renato
galliver, david
goldberg, reiner
grimaldi, giorgio
haefliger, ernst
heilmann, uwe
hollweg, werner
jerusalem, siegfried
kraus, alfredo

albanese, francesco
altmeyer, theo
araiza, francisco
blochwitz, hans-peter
bottion, aldo
campora, giuseppe
casellato, renzo
cioni, renato
cossutta, carlo
davies, arthur
di stefano, giuseppe
ellenbeck, dieter
feiersinger, sebastian
gedda, nicolai
gonzalez, dalmacio
grobe, donald
handt, herbert
hofmann, peter
hughes, david
konya, sandor
krenn, werner

tenors who appeared with carlo maria giulini/concluded

labo, flaviano	lanigan, john
laubenthal, horst	lavender, justin
lewis, keith	lewis, richard
lippert, herbert	luchetti, veriano
margison, richard	mercuriali, angelo
merigi, giorgio	miller, kevin
misciano, alvino	mitchinson, john
monti, nicola	moser, thomas
munteanu, petre	neate, ken
oncina, juan	ottolini, luigi
partridge, ian	pavarotti, luciano
pears, peter	penno, gino
poggi, gianni	prandelli, giacinto
prevedi, bruno	prior, beniamino
protschka, josef	raimondi, gianni
riegel, kenneth	schreier, peter
seiffert, peter	steinbach, heribert
tear, robert	trama, ugo
trost, rainer	valletti, cesare
vickers, jon	vroons, frans
winbergh, gösta	wohlers, rüdiger
young, alexander	zampieri, giuseppe
benelli, ugo	

baritones and basses who appeared with carlo maria giulini
singers of minor operatic roles are not included

allen, thomas
bailey, norman
berry, walter
borg, kim
bruson, renato
calabrese, franco
campi, enrico
cava, carlo
colombara, carlo
corena, fernando
crass, franz
desderi, claudio
el hage, robert
evans, geraint
fioravanti, giulio
flagello, ezio
furlanetto, ferruccio
ghiaurov, nicolai

arié, raffaele
bastianini, ettore
blanc, ernest
bruscantini, sesto
burchuladze, paata
cameron, john
capecchi, renato
christoff, boris
colzani, anselmo
cortis, marcello
dean, stafford
dondi, dino
estes, simon
ferrin, agostino
fischer-dieskau, dietrich
frick, gottlob
ganzarolli, vladimiro
gilfrey, rodney

baritones and basses who appeared with carlo maria giulini/concluded

glossop, peter	gobbi, tito
guelfi, carlo	guelfi, giangiacomo
gynrod, friedrich	hagegard, hakan
hale, robert	haugland, aage
hoekman, guus	holl, robert
howell, gwynne	kamann, karl
krause, tom	langdon, michael
lloyd, robert	luise, melchiorre
luxon, benjamin	macurdy, william
maionica, silvio	mascherini, enzo
massard, robert	mccue, william
mikulas, peter	miles, alastair
modesti, giuseppe	moll, kurt
monachesi, walter	monreale, leonardo
montarsolo, paolo	morris, james
nimsgern, siegmund	nucci, leo
panerai, rolando	pape, rené
petri, mario	poli, afro
plishka, paul	poell, alfred
prey, hermann	protti, aldo
raimondi, ruggiero	ramey, samuel
ridderbusch, karl	rintzler, marius
rootering, jan-hendrik	rossi-lemeni, nicola
rouleau, joseph	rydl, kurt
sardi, ivan	schmidt, andreas
shaw, john	shirley-quirk, john
siepi, cesare	silveri, paolo
sordello, enzo	sotin, hans
souzay, gérard	stamm, harald
stefanoni, marco	taddei, giuseppe
tadeo, giorgio	tagliabue, carlo
tajo, italo	talvela, martti
terfel, bryn	tozzi, giorgio
van dam, josé	vandenburg, howard
vinco, ivo	wächter, eberhard
ward, david	washington, paolo
weikl, bernd	welitsch, alexander
wilbrink, hans	wilson-johnson, david
zaccaria, nicola	paskalis, kostas

Music and Books published by Travis & Emery Music Bookshop:

Anon.: Hymnarium Sarisburiense, cum Rubricis et Notis Musicis.
Agricola, Johann Friedrich from Tosi: Anleitung zur Singkunst.
Bach, C.P.E.: edited W. Emery: Nekrolog or Obituary Notice of J.S. Bach.
Bateson, Naomi Judith: Alcock of Salisbury
Bathe, William: A Briefe Introduction to the Skill of Song (c.1587)
Bax, Arnold: Symphony #5, Arranged for Piano Four Hands by Walter Emery
Burney, Charles: The Present State of Music in France and Italy (1771)
Burney, Charles: The Present State of Music in Germany, Netherlands... (1773)
Burney, Charles: An Account of the Musical Performances ... Handel (1784)
Burney, Karl: Nachricht von Georg Friedrich Handel's Lebensumstanden (1784)
Burns, Robert: The Caledonian Musical Museum ... Best Scotch Songs (1810)
Cobbett, W.W.: Cobbett's Cyclopedic Survey of Chamber Music. (2 vols.)
Corrette, Michel: Le Maitre de Clavecin (1753)
Crimp, Bryan: Dear Mr. Rosenthal ... Dear Mr. Gaisberg ...
Crimp, Bryan: Solo: The Biography of Solomon
D'Indy, Vincent: Beethoven: Biographie Critique (in French, 1911)
D'Indy, Vincent: Beethoven: A Critical Biography (in English, 1912)
D'Indy, Vincent: César Franck (in French, 1910)
Fischhof, Joseph: Versuch einer Geschichte des Clavierbaues (1853).
Frescobaldi, Girolamo: D'Arie Musicali per Cantarsi. Primo & Secondo Libro.
Geminiani, Francesco: The Art of Playing the Violin (1751)
Handel; Purcell; Boyce et al: Calliope or English Harmony: Vol. First. (1746)
Häuser: Musikalisches Lexikon. 2 vols in one.
Hawkins, John: General History of the Science & Practice of Music (5 vols. 1776)
Herbert-Caesari, Edgar: The Science and Sensations of Vocal Tone
Herbert-Caesari, Edgar: Vocal Truth
Hopkins and Rimboult: The Organ. Its History and Construction.
Hunt, John: Adam to Webern: the recordings of von Karajan
Hunt, John: several discographies – see separate list.
Isaacs, Lewis: Hänsel and Gretel. A Guide to Humperdinck's Opera.
Isaacs, Lewis: Königskinder (Royal Children) A Guide to Humperdinck's Opera.
Kastner: Manuel Général de Musique Militaire
Lacassagne, M. l'Abbé Joseph : Traité Général des élémens du Chant.
Lascelles (née Catley), Anne: The Life of Miss Anne Catley.
Mainwaring, John: Memoirs of the Life of the Late George Frederic Handel
Malcolm, Alexander: A Treaty of Music: Speculative, Practical and Historical
Marx, Adolph Bernhard: Die Kunst des Gesanges, Theoretisch-Practisch (1826)
May, Florence: The Life of Brahms (2nd edition)
May, Florence: The Girlhood Of Clara Schumann: Clara Wieck And Her Time.
Mellers, Wilfrid: Angels of the Night: Popular Female Singers of Our Time
Mellers, Wilfrid: Bach and the Dance of God
Mellers, Wilfrid: Beethoven and the Voice of God
Mellers, Wilfrid: Caliban Reborn - Renewal in Twentieth Century Music

Music and Books published by Travis & Emery Music Bookshop:

Mellers, Wilfrid: François Couperin and the French Classical Tradition
Mellers, Wilfrid: Harmonious Meeting
Mellers, Wilfrid: Le Jardin Retrouvé, The Music of Frederic Mompou
Mellers, Wilfrid: Music and Society, England and the European Tradition
Mellers, Wilfrid: Music in a New Found Land: ... ... American Music
Mellers, Wilfrid: Romanticism and the Twentieth Century (from 1800)
Mellers, Wilfrid: The Masks of Orpheus: ...... the Story of European Music.
Mellers, Wilfrid: The Sonata Principle (from c. 1750)
Mellers, Wilfrid: Vaughan Williams and the Vision of Albion
Panchianio, Cattuffio: Rutzvanscad Il Giovine (1737)
Pearce, Charles: Sims Reeves, Fifty Years of Music in England.
Pettitt, Stephen: Philharmonia Orchestra: Complete Discography (1987)
Playford, John: An Introduction to the Skill of Musick (1674)
Purcell, Henry et al: Harmonia Sacra ... The First Book, (1726)
Purcell, Henry et al: Harmonia Sacra ... Book II (1726)
Quantz, Johann: Versuch einer Anweisung die Flöte traversiere zu spielen.
Rameau, Jean-Philippe: Code de Musique Pratique, ou Methodes (1760)
Rastall, Richard: The Notation of Western Music.
Rimbault, Edward: The Pianoforte, Its Origins, Progress, and Construction.
Rousseau, Jean Jacques: Dictionnaire de Musique
Rubinstein, Anton : Guide to the proper use of the Pianoforte Pedals.
Sainsbury, John S.: Dictionary of Musicians. Vol. 1. (1825). 2 vols.
Serré de Rieux, Jean de : Les dons des Enfans de Latone
Simpson, Christopher: A Compendium of Practical Musick in Five Parts
Spohr, Louis: Autobiography
Spohr, Louis: Grand Violin School
Tans'ur, William: A New Musical Grammar; or The Harmonical Spectator
Terry, Charles Sanford: John Christian Bach (Johann Christian Bach) (1929)
Terry, Charles Sanford: J.S. Bach's Original Hymn-Tunes for Congregational Use
Terry, Charles Sanford: Four-Part Chorals of J.S. Bach. (German & English)
Terry, Charles Sanford: Joh. Seb. Bach, Cantata Texts, Sacred and Secular.
Terry, Charles Sanford: The Origins of the Family of Bach Musicians.
Tosi, Pierfrancesco: Opinioni de' Cantori Antichi, e Moderni (1723)
Van der Straeten, Edmund: History of the Violoncello, The Viol da Gamba ...
Van der Straeten, Edmund: History of the Violin, Its Ancestors... (2 vols.)
Waltern: Musikalisches Lexicon
Walther, J. G.: Musicalisches Lexikon ober Musicalische Bibliothec

Travis & Emery Music Bookshop
17 Cecil Court, London, WC2N 4EZ, United Kingdom.
Tel. (+44) 20 7240 2129

© Travis & Emery 2009

Discographies by Travis & Emery:
Discographies by John Hunt.

1987: 978-1-906857-14-1: From Adam to Webern: the Recordings of von Karajan.

1991: 978-0-951026-83-0: 3 Italian Conductors and 7 Viennese Sopranos: 10 Discographies: Arturo Toscanini, Guido Cantelli, Carlo Maria Giulini, Elisabeth Schwarzkopf, Irmgard Seefried, Elisabeth Gruemmer, Sena Jurinac, Hilde Gueden, Lisa Della Casa, Rita Streich.

1992: 978-0-951026-85-4: Mid-Century Conductors and More Viennese Singers: 10 Discographies: Karl Boehm, Victor De Sabata, Hans Knappertsbusch, Tullio Serafin, Clemens Krauss, Anton Dermota, Leonie Rysanek, Eberhard Waechter, Maria Reining, Erich Kunz.

1993: 978-0-951026-87-8: More 20th Century Conductors: 7 Discographies: Eugen Jochum, Ferenc Fricsay, Carl Schuricht, Felix Weingartner, Josef Krips, Otto Klemperer, Erich Kleiber.

1994: 978-0-951026-88-5: Giants of the Keyboard: 6 Discographies: Wilhelm Kempff, Walter Gieseking, Edwin Fischer, Clara Haskil, Wilhelm Backhaus, Artur Schnabel.

1994: 978-0-951026-89-2: Six Wagnerian Sopranos: 6 Discographies: Frieda Leider, Kirsten Flagstad, Astrid Varnay, Martha Moedl, Birgit Nilsson, Gwyneth Jones.

1995: 978-0-952582-70-0: Musical Knights: 6 Discographies: Henry Wood, Thomas Beecham, Adrian Boult, John Barbirolli, Reginald Goodall, Malcolm Sargent.

1995: 978-0-952582-71-7: A Notable Quartet: 4 Discographies: Gundula Janowitz, Christa Ludwig, Nicolai Gedda, Dietrich Fischer-Dieskau.

1996: 978-0-952582-72-4: The Post-War German Tradition: 5 Discographies: Rudolf Kempe, Joseph Keilberth, Wolfgang Sawallisch, Rafael Kubelik, Andre Cluytens.

1996: 978-0-952582-73-1: Teachers and Pupils: 7 Discographies: Elisabeth Schwarzkopf, Maria Ivoguen, Maria Cebotari, Meta Seinemeyer, Ljuba Welitsch, Rita Streich, Erna Berger.

1996: 978-0-952582-77-9: Tenors in a Lyric Tradition: 3 Discographies: Peter Anders, Walther Ludwig, Fritz Wunderlich.

1997: 978-0-952582-78-6: The Lyric Baritone: 5 Discographies: Hans Reinmar, Gerhard Huesch, Josef Metternich, Hermann Uhde, Eberhard Waechter.

1997: 978-0-952582-79-3: Hungarians in Exile: 3 Discographies: Fritz Reiner, Antal Dorati, George Szell.

1997: 978-1-901395-00-6: The Art of the Diva: 3 Discographies: Claudia Muzio, Maria Callas, Magda Olivero.

1997: 978-1-901395-01-3: Metropolitan Sopranos: 4 Discographies: Rosa Ponselle, Eleanor Steber, Zinka Milanov, Leontyne Price.

1997: 978-1-901395-02-0: Back From The Shadows: 4 Discographies: Willem Mengelberg, Dimitri Mitropoulos, Hermann Abendroth, Eduard Van Beinum.

1997: 978-1-901395-03-7: More Musical Knights: 4 Discographies: Hamilton Harty, Charles Mackerras, Simon Rattle, John Pritchard.

1998: 978-1-901395-94-5: Conductors On The Yellow Label: 8 Discographies: Fritz Lehmann, Ferdinand Leitner, Ferenc Fricsay, Eugen Jochum, Leopold Ludwig, Artur Rother, Franz Konwitschny, Igor Markevitch.

1998: 978-1-901395-95-2: More Giants of the Keyboard: 5 Discographies: Claudio Arrau, Gyorgy Cziffra, Vladimir Horowitz, Dinu Lipatti, Artur Rubinstein.

1998: 978-1-901395-96-9: Mezzo and Contraltos: 5 Discographies: Janet Baker, Margarete Klose, Kathleen Ferrier, Giulietta Simionato, Elisabeth Hoengen.

1999: 978-1-901395-97-6: The Furtwaengler Sound Sixth Edition: Discography and Concert Listing.
1999: 978-1-901395-98-3: The Great Dictators: 3 Discographies: Evgeny Mravinsky, Artur Rodzinski, Sergiu Celibidache.
1999: 978-1-901395-99-0: Sviatoslav Richter: Pianist of the Century: Discography.
2000: 978-1-901395-04-4: Philharmonic Autocrat 1: Discography of: Herbert Von Karajan [Third Edition].
2000: 978-1-901395-05-1: Wiener Philharmoniker 1 - Vienna Philharmonic and Vienna State Opera Orchestras: Discography Part 1 1905-1954.
2000: 978-1-901395-06-8: Wiener Philharmoniker 2 - Vienna Philharmonic and Vienna State Opera Orchestras: Discography Part 2 1954-1989.
2001: 978-1-901395-07-5: Gramophone Stalwarts: 3 Separate Discographies: Bruno Walter, Erich Leinsdorf, Georg Solti.
2001: 978-1-901395-08-2: Singers of the Third Reich: 5 Discographies: Helge Roswaenge, Tiana Lemnitz, Franz Voelker, Maria Mueller, Max Lorenz.
2001: 978-1-901395-09-9: Philharmonic Autocrat 2: Concert Register of Herbert Von Karajan Second Edition.
2002: 978-1-901395-10-5: Sächsische Staatskapelle Dresden: Complete Discography.
2002: 978-1-901395-11-2: Carlo Maria Giulini: Discography and Concert Register.
2002: 978-1-901395-12-9: Pianists For The Connoisseur: 6 Discographies: Arturo Benedetti Michelangeli, Alfred Cortot, Alexis Weissenberg, Clifford Curzon, Solomon, Elly Ney.
2003: 978-1-901395-14-3: Singers on the Yellow Label: 7 Discographies: Maria Stader, Elfriede Troetschel, Annelies Kupper, Wolfgang Windgassen, Ernst Haefliger, Josef Greindl, Kim Borg.
2003: 978-1-901395-15-0: A Gallic Trio: 3 Discographies: Charles Muench, Paul Paray, Pierre Monteux.
2004: 978-1-901395-16-7: Antal Dorati 1906-1988: Discography and Concert Register.
2004: 978-1-901395-17-4: Columbia 33CX Label Discography.
2004: 978-1-901395-18-1: Great Violinists: 3 Discographies: David Oistrakh, Wolfgang Schneiderhan, Arthur Grumiaux.
2006: 978-1-901395-19-8: Leopold Stokowski: Second Edition of the Discography.
2006: 978-1-901395-20-4: Wagner Im Festspielhaus: Discography of the Bayreuth Festival.
2006: 978-1-901395-21-1: Her Master's Voice: Concert Register and Discography of Dame Elisabeth Schwarzkopf [Third Edition].
2007: 978-1-901395-22-8: Hans Knappertsbusch: Kna: Concert Register and Discography of Hans Knappertsbusch, 1888-1965. Second Edition.
2008: 978-1-901395-23-5: Philips Minigroove: Second Extended Version of the European Discography.
2009: 978-1-901395--24-2: American Classics: The Discographies of Leonard Bernstein and Eugene Ormandy.

Discography by Stephen J. Pettitt, edited by John Hunt:
1987: 978-1-906857-16-5: Philharmonia Orchestra: Complete Discography 1945-1987

Available from: Travis & Emery at 17 Cecil Court, London, UK. (+44) 20 7 240 2129. email on sales@travis-and-emery.com .

© Travis & Emery 2009

www.ingramcontent.com/pod-product-compliance
Lightning Source LLC
Chambersburg PA
CBHW052102230426
43671CB00011B/1907